*When Grief Became My Gift:*
*40 Days of Gentle Healing*

*By Rayna Piazza*

*When Grief Became My Gift: 40 Days of Gentle Healing Devotional*
Copyright © 2025 Rayna Piazza
www.raynasbooks.com
Cover Design: Sarah Geringer
Editor: Sarah Geringer
ISBN: 979-8-9932612-1-8

Unless otherwise indicated, all Scripture quotations are from The Passion Translation®. Copyright © 2017, 2018, 2020 by Passion & Fire Ministries, Inc. Used by permission. All rights reserved. ThePassionTranslation.com.

Please note that the author's publishing style capitalizes certain pronouns in Scripture that refer to Father God, Son, and Holy Spirit and may differ from other publishers' styles.

# Dedication

I dedicate this devotional to all the incredible people who stood by me without judgment during the aftermath of my sudden loss. To everyone who brought meals to our home, folded my laundry, washed my dishes, flew in or drove long distances for the funeral, loved on my kids, and sat with me on the sofa speaking encouraging words as I cried. I am forever grateful.

I especially dedicate this devotional to my three children who have persisted on despite the incredible loss of their father. You three are true heroes. I love each of you a million times a million.

Finally, I dedicate this book to everyone who has faced unimaginable pain. Thank you for trusting me with your emotional pain. Jesus faithfully healed my heart, and I know he will do the same for you. I have covered these words in prayer and intercession with the Holy Spirit. May you step into freedom from emotional pain and fulfill your God-given destiny, regardless of what life has thrown at you. Far greater is God that is in you than the evil that is in the world.

*"Little children, you can be certain that you belong to God and have conquered them, for the One who is living in you is far greater than the one who is in the world."*
*1 John 4:4*

# Table of Contents

# Disclaimer

This devotional and its activations for gentle healing from grief are not intended for medical conditions like clinical depression, among others, although they may help. I wrote "When Grief Became My Gift" for anyone dealing with the aftermath of sudden loss.

I share my experience with genuine hope that it will encourage others to pursue Jesus and allow him to heal their hearts through God's Word and by engaging with the Spirit of God. This devotional aims to provide practical steps and heartfelt prayers to help all who read it find personal emotional healing and live a beautiful, fulfilled life.

I am not a medical doctor. The content of this devotional is for spiritual encouragement and personal reflection only. Please do not stop or change any prescribed medications or treatments without first consulting your healthcare provider.

# How It All Started

Grief hit me in the most shocking way, which I imagine is its usual path. I was planning dinner and then driving to pick up my son when something felt off. My husband, Brett, hadn't returned my three phone calls that day. We had an agreement that if one of us called twice, the other had to call back because it meant "we need to talk." I was on the third call, then the fourth.

I had tracked his phone all afternoon, and I knew the exact doctor's office where he was located. The weird part was that he had been in the same spot for several hours. As a medical device sales rep, this was not like him because he usually spent about half an hour at each office. He was about 30 miles away, so I decided to drive there. What I found changed my and my children's lives forever.

My husband took his own life in his car that summer afternoon. I was the first one to find him, and I went into shock. I called 9-1-1, and then my nightmare began. I stepped into a world that did not include my best friend. It was slowly sinking in that my husband was never coming back on this side of heaven.

I couldn't catch my breath, even though I was breathing fine. I wanted to scream, but only a tear rolled down my cheek as I answered the detective's questions. I kept running to the grass by the parking lot, feeling like I needed to vomit, but nothing would come up. I felt both numb and overwhelmed with emotion. It was as if I was running and standing still at the same time. I kept trying to speak, but the words wouldn't come out. Apparently, I was in shock. With the help of my precious sister and dear friends, I made it back home that day.

## Coping with Sudden Loss

In the aftermath, we had an outpouring of love from our family and friends. I will always hold those precious conversations and the compassion expressed from our loved ones close to my heart. The kindness, generosity, and love of our community showed up in every way possible. I am so grateful to have had so much support.

All of our family and friends were just as shocked as I was by my husband's suicide. Still, none of us could undo what he did. Death is so final.

Once the funeral was over, I wanted nothing to do with the grief. I hated the constant crying and sadness. As a mom to a toddler, I felt guilty for crying all the time. She needed me to be happy.

I had all these nagging questions in my heart that kept presenting themselves repeatedly. It was like a hamster wheel of regret. Can't we just go back to the happy days? Why didn't God heal my husband from his ailments? What do I truly believe about God and his love?

God showed me very gently that he did heal my husband, and every prayer I prayed for him was answered. It just wasn't the way I thought it would happen. My husband is now in heaven without the physical and emotional pain of life.

## When My Grief Journey Began to Feel Meaningful

I slowly realized during my grief journey that Father God was now using my grief to heal me. This hidden gift of tears slowly soothed my broken heart. The grief was a gift that I had the choice to accept or reject. I was learning that I am still deeply loved by Father God despite my intense feelings of grief, anger, and sadness. The overflow of emotion was an invitation from Jesus to heal my heart. He wanted me to examine the difficult aspects of my life, and he was pursuing me to provide me with answers.

My emotional pain was surfacing from the unhealthy parts of my soul that needed healing. The soul consists of our mind, will, and emotions. Jesus was using my sudden grief as the catalyst for the negative belief systems in my heart. My pain was this open door, allowing me to pause and think about my thoughts. This encounter with grief opened the door to every hurt I had ever endured throughout my entire life. I felt overwhelmed, shocked, and like I was on a rollercoaster of unwanted memories and emotions.

The process of emotional healing begins in the mind. Did you know that your thoughts drive all your emotions? You can't experience an emotion without first having a thought. Our conscious and subconscious thoughts create a belief system. When our belief system is distorted, it causes emotional pain. To understand where I was on my journey, I had to ask myself, "What do I truly believe about myself, my faith, my life, and my future?"

Grief brings both your conscious and subconscious thoughts and beliefs to the surface. To me, the grief felt like a gushing river of emotions I couldn't stop, no matter how hard I tried, because the water kept finding a way to bust through in the oddest of places. Every barrier I had in place to protect myself was ripped wide open.

My worst nightmare was unfolding right before my eyes. I felt guilty and responsible, then angry and even relieved. I hated the emotions because they felt so raw and out of control. I was mad, then I was extremely sad. I would reminisce and feel so loved, then realize that my world was turned upside down and start bawling again.

**My New Reality Began to Sink In**

I was surprised by how deep my emotions ran. Everything felt unfamiliar and new because I had to face life without my spouse. I went to the extreme of believing that every dream we shared as a couple had to die since he would not be there to experience it with me. But then I would come back to my senses and realize that I could honor my husband and still chase our dreams.

As the grief rolled over me, I would go through extreme highs remembering the good times, and then a fallout when my reality hit me again. I blamed myself, thinking I should have saved my husband. I beat myself up for not knowing his plan to take his own life. Then I would come back to the realization that I didn't have the power to save him because

9

he was a grown man with his own free will. It was not my fault, even though most of the time it felt like it was.

The flood of emotions was overwhelming, to say the least. Everything I thought and believed was being crushed. Initially, the grief was this constant, unsettling group of feelings that rocked my foundation to its core. It was something from which I couldn't escape. As I started to accept it, the grief became a part of me.

I understood from years of counseling that if I wanted a different feeling, I needed a different belief, but not just any belief. It had to be a belief that aligned with the truth of God's Word. I knew I had to change my beliefs, but my thoughts felt so out of control. I couldn't calm down long enough to identify my conscious thinking, much less access my subconscious thoughts. Eventually, I let my heart settle and gave my emotions the space they needed. I allowed myself to feel my feelings and ponder the crazy thoughts flooding my mind instead of running away from them.

Oddly enough, in the midst of my emotional pain and feeling super crazy, I felt securely loved by Jesus. I was having this out-of-body experience, feeling like this wasn't my life. My heart couldn't accept that my husband was gone forever. I felt like he would walk back through the front door and make a joke to everyone there. It might sound crazy, but that's how it felt.

## God's Tangible Presence

As much as I felt out of control, I had a deep knowing in my heart that we were going to be okay. I didn't know how, but the peace of God kept settling deep within me. There were so many people praying for us, and I knew Jesus was answering their cries. I could feel the tangible presence of God.

Comfort and compassion from the Holy Spirit were residing in my heart from the time I woke up to when I closed my eyes at night. Deep down in my core, I knew my Father God was going to take care of us; it was a knowing and not a feeling. I was immersed in the love of God, but I still felt so much pain.

Emotions serve as guides to the pain hidden within our hearts. They reveal our true beliefs; however, they are not always dependable indicators of the truth. Feeling hopeless doesn't mean my life will always lack hope.

The key is to find a balance by acknowledging the painful emotions rather than suppressing them, so they can function as a helpful guide to uncover our belief system. Then, as it says in Romans 12:2, we can be transformed by the renewing of our minds. We counteract the negative beliefs with the truth of God's Word.

Grief awakens these hidden places of emotional pain that were always present but concealed. As each of these deep feelings surfaced in my heart, I could do nothing but hand them over to Jesus one by one. I felt this relentless surge of anger, fear, and pain.

I knew deep in my soul that the tragedy I was facing would produce good fruit. I also knew it was going to take time because there were so many feelings and thought patterns to unpack. In this process, I started to understand the gift of my grief because I knew without a doubt that my Father God wanted to heal these hurt places within me.

For the record, I am not saying that losing my husband to suicide is a gift. It is and always will be a tragedy. However, the emotions and thought patterns I was able to access from the grief are truly a gift because I was able to look at my pain from a different perspective for the first time in years. No longer could I look away and pretend like it was not there.

## When Grief Became My Gift

Grief became a gift to me because it opened a new path to healing. As I mentioned before, I believe that God gave us our emotions as a guide. When something hurts my heart, I feel it is Jesus knocking on my door, saying, "Can I heal this part of you? Let's look at your pain, my sweet girl."

Grief comes in many forms and is certainly not limited to mourning the death of a loved one. You might be grieving a breakup, dealing with a divorce, facing a serious health diagnosis, coping with an estranged adult child, or reacting to the discovery of infidelity in your marriage, just to name a few.

Without grief, I never would have found a way to process my emotional pain. It gave a voice to the suffering and struggles within my heart. Are you willing to allow your grief to have its own space in your heart?

If we let it, grief can be a gateway to the places where we need deep, emotional healing. We can offer our pain as a sacrifice to Father God, and he exchanges it for healing. *The true gift is the healing*. The path to get there is recognizing and acknowledging where we hurt and why.

## My Inspiration

The sudden, tragic loss I experienced from my husband's suicide threw me into a cycle of grief that inspired this devotional. My grief was so big and loud that I had to face it. I knew my life would never recover had I not dealt with my heart, and I want to share with you how I learned to receive my grief as a gift.

Will grief be your anchor to darkness or your catalyst for healing? The beauty of this question is that when you are ready, you get to decide your path and whether or not you choose to heal. It's no longer about what happened to you but about the choices you now have as a person with your future laid out before you. I want to show you how Jesus gently showed me how to choose healing. I hope it will encourage you to trust him and receive your personal healing.

## Prayer

*Father God,*

*Lead me and guide me in my grief journey. Open my heart to receive your love in a new way. Give me hope to believe for my future. Grant me your peace to tackle all the questions that arise. I ask for your wisdom to partner with me and lead the way.*

*Ground me in your love. Allow me to see you and hear you in everything I do and in every part of my day. Heal me, Father God, and make me whole again. I ask you to prepare me for and catapult me into my God-given destiny.*

*In Jesus' name, I pray,*
*Amen*

# Quick Tips Before You Get Started

- When the reflection questions and activations ask you about negative emotions, refer to Appendix A (List of Negative Emotions & The Opposite Positive Emotions) in the back of the devotional.

- **Before you start Day 1, please read Appendix B** (How to Use Your Imagination to See God) in the back of the devotional. It provides detailed directions for getting the most out of the activations.

- If a particular declaration resonates deeply with you, I strongly suggest committing 60 days to speaking it out loud over your life and then imagining God releasing that truth over you while feeling the positive emotion of the declaration. This will help retrain your brain to adopt positive mindsets.

- I keep a note in my phone with my current declarations, including the start date, which helps me keep track of the 60 days.

# Day 1

🔥

## *Lead Me to You, God*

*"God, I invite your searching gaze into my heart. Examine me through and through; find out everything that may be hidden within me. Put me to the test and sift through all my anxious cares. See if there is any path of pain I'm walking on, and lead me back to your glorious, everlasting way—the path that brings me back to you."*
*Psalm 139:23-24*

The pain of losing my husband to suicide didn't start the day he took his life. It was poking at me long before that dreadful day. My husband, Brett, was a chronic pain patient. Sixteen years prior, his car was hit by an 18-wheeler going 45 miles per hour while he was at a dead stop. The injuries Brett suffered were intense, causing him to be on and off pain medication and depression medication throughout our entire marriage.

We were married for nine years, and we had issues just like everyone else. However, the issues felt so much bigger when I had to face the public shame of his suicide. My life's pain was on display for everyone to see, and it felt so heavy.

Suicide exposes pain, and it feels like it is out there for everyone to see and judge. It's a vulnerable place, and it hurts. I struggled with how our children would handle it long-term and how I would recover. Would life ever look the same? The future seemed bleak and uncertain.

Dealing with the sudden loss of my husband triggered the many places of pain in my heart. It revealed these hidden doors that opened me up to fear, rejection, and abandonment. I very much felt "put to the test" just as it says in Psalm 139:23. There were so many fears in my heart that I had apparently been suppressing my entire life. They were fears I didn't think I had, until that day.

Losing my husband, Brett, changed my perspective in so many ways. The only good thing I could see emerging from my heartache was that I no longer wanted to ignore the emotional pain in my life. I decided to finally surrender to the pain knocking on my heart's doors. I started by praying Psalm 139:23-24.

Will you invite Jesus in to search your heart and surrender your pain to him? I believe he's patiently waiting for our yes.

**Reflection Questions**
What anxious cares and fears are you carrying?


What path of pain are you walking? Explain your grief to Jesus.


What areas of your life are being put to the test?


**Declarations**
• I am being led back to Jesus and his glorious, everlasting way.
• Jesus is rescuing me.
• Grief will no longer rule my life in a negative way.

**Activation**
Picture yourself sitting with Father God on a picnic blanket in an open meadow. Give God permission to reveal the emotional pain hidden in your heart. Write down two or three specific heart pains that he shows to you. Describe the particular situation surrounding each instance of heart pain and the negative emotions you feel when recalling it. You can use Appendix A in the back of the devotional for a list of negative emotions and their opposites. Ask God to guide you back to the path that leads to him.

**My Heart Today** *(journal your thoughts below)*

**Prayer**

*Father God,*

*I invite you to search my heart. Examine me thoroughly and don't leave any door unopened. I give you permission to show me every hidden thing in my heart. Put me to the test because I know the fruit of your tests is always good. Uncover each one of my anxious feelings and thoughts. I ask you to reveal my own heart to me because I know you want to heal me.*

*Show me what I don't see on my path of emotional pain and grief. I want to partner with you. Set me on your path that brings me back to you. Lead me back to your glorious, everlasting way. I want to be healed, to serve you, and to walk in your glory for all of my days. Let it start today. Teach me your ways, Father God.*

*In Jesus' name, I pray,*
*Amen*

# Day 2

🪶

## *The Fiery Love of God*

*"When I screamed out, 'Lord, I'm doomed!' your fiery love was stirred, and you raced to my rescue. Whenever my busy thoughts were out of control, the soothing comfort of your presence calmed me down and overwhelmed me with delight."*
*Psalm 94:18-19*

The early days after Brett's suicide were brutal. I was up and down in my emotions. There was no longer a facade allowing me to act like everything was okay. The grief hit me in waves. The immense loss covered me like a blanket. I had so many questions.

Brett was my best friend, no matter what we faced. He had struggled, but he was also in an extraordinary amount of pain each day. The pain produced stress, and it felt like a force we could never control.

I truly believe my husband was convinced I was better off without him. It feels insane to write that. The mere thought of the love of my life believing that lie crushes my heart. I truly felt doomed, like it says in Psalm 94:18. When the Holy Spirit led me to read Psalm 94, my heart started to calm down.

I realized that my feelings of doom and devastation stirred Father God's fiery love for me. The God of the universe was racing to my rescue. I started to calm down as the revelation of this verse sank into my heart. I could feel God all around me, and his love was tangibly touching me at my every turn.

God's presence was so noticeable in my season of grief. Each problem I faced kept miraculously working out. My affairs turned out to be taken care of despite my intense fear of losing everything. As my thoughts would spiral, the Holy Spirit would calm me down with God's Word. Psalm 94:19 comforted me with these words, "The soothing comfort of Your presence calmed me down and overwhelmed me with delight."

Brett and I had created a beautiful life together. Facing the fact that he would never be there to enjoy it with me felt devastating. Despite it all, I knew deep in my heart that my children and I were going to be okay. Although I had no idea how everything would work out, for the first time in my life, I was okay with that.

### Reflection Questions
What negative thoughts are running through your mind? If you can't think of any right now, sit with the question and wait for the answer.


Are you comfortable trusting Jesus with your future, even if you don't know everything? If not, write down the areas where you feel uncomfortable.



### Declarations
- My feelings of doom and devastation stir up Father God's fiery love for me.
- Father God is racing to my rescue.
- I trust Jesus to heal my grief and set me free from being ruled by negative emotions.

### Activation
Have you ever considered that your pain awakens Father God's love for you? Keep that in mind and close your eyes. Imagine Father God running toward you to rescue you, then hugging you when he reaches you. Let his love flow freely through your body as you feel his embrace. Ask Father God what he wants to say about the grief you've experienced and write down his response.

**My Heart Today**

**Prayer**

*Father God,*

*I am crying out to you in my pain. I feel doomed and devastated. As I call out to you, please meet with me. Sit with me and teach me your ways. Stir up your fiery love in my heart. I receive the fact that you are racing to my rescue, and I give you permission to rescue me.*

*I choose to look for you in every part of my life. Show me where you are. I ask you to silence my spiraling thoughts. Fill my heart up with your soothing comfort to calm me down. Show me how to experience you and your presence above all else. Overwhelm me with your delight.*

*In Jesus' name, I pray,*
*Amen*

# Day 3

*Entwining My Heart with Yahweh*

*"But those who entwine their hearts with YAHWEH will experience divine strength. They will rise up on soaring wings and fly like eagles, run their races without growing weary, and walk through life without giving up."*
*Isaiah 40:31*

Most mornings, I wake up early, brew a cup of coffee, and journal with Jesus. In fact, most of the revelations in these pages come from my journaling sessions with Jesus. I have also heard this kind of journaling is called two-way prayer. You write your prayer in your journal, then wait and listen. When Jesus responds to your heart, you write down his words. It's one of the most beautiful experiences I have ever had.

My journaling has led me to a place where my heart is deeply entwined with Jesus. As I abide in communion with the Lord, I listen for his voice. Then I write down everything I'm hearing. I usually start with a scripture like Isaiah 40:31 to remind me of his promises and the incredible depth of his glory.

The promise of Isaiah 40:31 alone blows my mind. To think that all I need to do is sit with Jesus and I will experience divine strength. Through Christ in me, I can rise up, run my race without weariness, and walk through life without giving up. I meditate on these words in scripture, then I imagine Jesus sitting next to me. It's the primary way I have navigated my grief.

In the early days of losing my husband, I couldn't imagine sitting with Jesus and journaling again. But gradually, I was able to get there and rebuild my trust in his voice. One of the first questions I asked him was why he didn't tell me that day that Brett was going to die. Jesus responded to me with this conversation:

*"Would you tell your child that their spouse was going to die that day, knowing it could not be prevented? Or would you be right there with them, as close as you could be, to let them fall into your arms?"*

Jesus chose to let me fall into his arms. He's been by my side all along. Will you try sitting with Jesus, listening to his voice, and writing down what you perceive? I promise you'll never be the same in the best way.

We were created to hear the voice of Jesus and for him to be our shepherd. My journaling has been based on this scripture:

*"My own sheep will hear my voice and I know each one, and they will follow me."*
*John 10:27*

The Holy Spirit speaks to you through God's Word. Look what it says here:

*"For the Holy Spirit makes God's fatherhood real to us as he whispers into our innermost being, 'You are God's beloved child!'"*
*Romans 8:16-17*

The Holy Spirit whispers to us into our innermost being. Isn't that beautiful? I encourage you to journal with Jesus by sitting quietly, seeking him, and writing down what you hear in your heart.

**Reflection Questions**
What do you want to talk to Jesus about today?


Do you believe he will respond to you? Why or why not?

What hard questions do you have for Jesus?

## Declarations
- I will rise up on soaring wings and fly like an eagle.
- My grief season will come to an end and I am strengthened for my life ahead.
- I entwine my heart with Father God and I experience divine strength.
- I run my race without growing weary.
- I am confident, and I walk through life without giving up.

## Activation
Choose one of the hard questions you have for Jesus and present it to him. Imagine yourself sitting on a blanket in an open field with beautiful flowers in the distance and a light breeze flowing in the air. Breathe in the beauty all around you and ask Jesus to answer your question. Write down his response. Sit with him and entwine your heart with his. Share your answer from Jesus with a trusted friend for support.

## My Heart Today

## Prayer

*Father God,*

*Thank you that I can hear your voice through your Word. I feel so loved knowing that you love me. I choose to follow you for all of my days. Thank you for your promises in Isaiah 40:31.*

*I have decided to entwine my heart with you and experience divine strength. Teach me how to perceive your voice so I can rise up, run my race without weariness, and walk through my life without giving up. Thank you for all your encouragement in my life. I want more of you. Show me your ways because I want to be like you.*

*In Jesus' name, I pray,*
*Amen*

# Day 4

###### Fixing My Heart on God

*"Keep trusting in the Lord and do what is right in his eyes. Fix your heart on the promises of God, and you will dwell in the land, feasting on his faithfulness. Find your delight and true pleasure in YAHWEH, and he will give you what you desire the most."*
*Psalm 37:3-4*

About a month after my husband's death, I woke up thinking about God's faithfulness. I was trying to reconcile the two sides of my situation. On one hand, I would never see my husband again, and that felt beyond hopeless. On the other hand, I have three children who need to see hope despite their father's death. As a mother, I was not going to let my kids down, but I struggled to find my strength.

How can a faithful God allow such tragedy? The first answer is that the tragedy of my husband's suicide was not God's fault, nor do I believe that it was God's plan. Man operates in free will, and as a result of that, many things happen that are not within God's plan or purpose for our lives.

Brett's choice to take his own life was not God's perfect plan. God gave him free will, and he committed suicide. As devastated as I was by this new reality, I realized that I had a choice. I can either wallow in the pain and let it consume me, or I can keep trusting Jesus with all of my unanswered questions.

My grief journey led me into this place where I had no control. It was horrifying and exhilarating at the same time. I had unknowingly fought against losing control my entire life. Now I'm only just discovering that relinquishing control is the key to learning more about Jesus and stepping into deeper union with him. As unsettling as it felt, I kept running toward this newfound territory of the unknown because I could feel Jesus unlocking his mysteries and setting me free.

At that moment, I chose to focus on the faithfulness of God, realizing his ways are higher than my ways (Isaiah 55:9). I started to accept the truth that my life is happening for me and not to me. Even though being a widow was not what I would choose, I have the potential to thrive on this path. I am realizing that I can survive the suicide of my spouse and become whole again by focusing my heart on the promises of God.

As I began to choose faith over doubt, my grief seemed to lift. It wasn't all at once by any means. But there was a lighter side to me.

I invite you to stop doubting God's love for you. Embrace the unknown by accepting the fact that some things are completely beyond your control. In the end, you can trust Jesus with everything. Let's learn together how to focus on the truth of God's promises and his faithfulness.

**Reflection Questions**
Where are places in your life that you feel you have no control?


How can you shift your perspective to see that your life is happening for you, rather than to you?


In what situations are you doubting God's love for you?


What are God's promises for your life?

## Declarations
- I relinquish control and step into deeper union with Jesus.
- I choose to receive God's love for me.
- I feast on God's faithfulness every day.
- I find my delight and truly enjoy my relationship with God.

## Activation
Fix your heart on God's promises for your life. Say each one out loud and with authority. Picture yourself receiving each promise from Jesus. If you are holding on to unforgiveness toward God because of your situation, forgive him.

As a prophetic act, write down on a piece of paper the situation over which you have no control. For me, it would be never seeing my husband again. Then, burn that paper as a symbol of relinquishing control and stepping into a journey of trusting Jesus.

## My Heart Today

## Prayer

*Father God,*

*I repent for doubting you, and I relinquish control. I trust you and receive your love. I take true pleasure in knowing how much I am loved by you. I choose to focus on your delight and all the ways you have rescued me over the years. I boldly come before your throne of grace (Hebrews 4:16), and I ask you to give me the desires of my heart (Psalm 37:4).*

*Teach me how to hope and dream again, and show me how to do what is right in your eyes. I choose to trust you with my unknowns and my questions. Guide me as I learn how to feast on your faithfulness and fix my heart on God's promises.*

*In Jesus' name, I pray,*
*Amen*

# Day 5

### Trusting God

*"Give God the right to direct your life, and as you trust him along the way, you'll find he pulled it off perfectly! He will appear as your righteousness, as sure as the dawning of a new day. He will manifest as your justice, as sure and strong as the noonday sun."*
*Psalm 37:5-6*

On the second or third day after Brett went to heaven, I started to respond to the many heartfelt texts I was receiving from my family and friends. So many of our loved ones were reaching out, and that felt very encouraging. But, each time I responded, my heart would shatter with the realization that Brett was not coming back. My reality kept slapping me in the face, even though I was deeply moved to hear from each of these precious people in my life. As I opened each "I'm so sorry" text, I would respond with, "I am heartbroken."

One morning, while I was in the shower, I heard the Holy Spirit speak to me. It was about the texts I was responding to on my phone and how each time I texted the words, "I am heartbroken," it felt as if my heart was breaking again. The words were a declaration over my heart, and each time I texted them, deep emotions of fear, betrayal, rejection, and abandonment overwhelmed me.

Hot tears streamed down my cheeks, and my heart truly felt as if it were breaking. My face clenched in pain as I took in my new reality under the lens of hopelessness. I kept covering my face with my hands, and my whole body felt tense and unsure.

As I was crying and warm water was flowing over my head in the shower that day, I heard the Holy Spirit say, "You are not heartbroken, you are heart healing. If you'll let me, I will completely heal your heart."

I responded with, "Yes, Lord, I will let you." Then he said, "Stop texting and believing that your heart is broken. Your heart is healing, and there is pain in the healing process. You are in a temporary place of pain because I am healing your heart. Will you trust me?"

That morning in the shower, I chose to give God the right to direct my life. I stepped out of the shower and began worshipping Jesus despite my pain. I lifted both hands to him and sang, "I will trust you, my king."

I decided to put my trust in him with my grief, even though I still felt as though I didn't have many answers. I started to believe that my heart was healing instead of breaking. This revelation from the Holy Spirit changed the path of my grief journey. I found hope. My response to the texts changed to, "Thank you for your prayers. We can feel them."

The simple act of watching our words can change everything. The Holy Spirit corrected me for my good. Ironically, as I changed my response, my emotions began to change. A seed of hope was planted in my heart, and I was able to worship again. Isn't it amazing that such a simple conversation from the Holy Spirit can completely change our direction? I was encouraged by his words and then acted on the Holy Spirit's direction.

Is there something you keep saying about your grief that keeps you trapped in pain? Give it to Jesus and let him heal your heart.

**Reflection Questions**
What are the areas in your life where you are not trusting God?

What statements or texts are you saying that are keeping you trapped in pain?

In what areas of your life do you want Jesus to be your justice?

## Declarations
- I give God the right to direct my life.
- My heart is exponentially healing from the emotional pain I have experienced.
- My heart pain is temporary because I am choosing to align myself with the truth of God's Word.
- I am heart healing.

## Activation
Get a piece of paper and draw a line down the middle. On the left, list the statements or texts you've made/said that align with staying trapped in your pain. In my situation, it would be, "I am heartbroken." Focus on the truth that Jesus is your justice in this world. Yield to him and give him the right to direct your life.

Then, on the right side of the page, write down what Jesus says about that statement. For me, it would be "I am heart healing." Take a deep breath and listen for Jesus' response. Then, add the statements from the right side of the page to your declarations.

## My Heart Today

## Prayer

*Father God,*

*I choose to trust you and give you permission to direct my life. I'm sorry for texting and saying negative words that do not reflect your truth for my life. Will you forgive me? I ask you to become my righteousness, leading me in your ways. I ask you to manifest as my justice and heal all the suffering tied to my grief. I truly believe you can help me heal my life completely, despite what I am facing.*

*In Jesus' name, I pray,*
*Amen*

# Day 6

## Quieting Your Heart

*"Quiet your heart in his presence and wait patiently for YAHWEH.
And don't think for a moment that the wicked, in their prosperity, are
better off than you. Stay away from anger and revenge. Keep envy far
from you, for it only leads you into lies."*
*Psalm 37:7-8*

In the months that followed my husband's death, I found it extremely difficult to quiet my heart. I felt no patience to wait for God. My grief overtook every area of my life.

I felt like I had missed God because my entire ministry was about emotional healing, and the one person I wanted to be healed the most had taken his own life. It seemed like the antithesis of everything I lived for was happening to me. My husband, the man I waited for and trusted Jesus to bring into my life, left this world by his own choice. It felt like the ultimate betrayal.

Why could my husband not fight for us? I don't know if I'll ever get the answer to that question on this side of heaven. Psalm 37:8 struck a chord in my heart when it said, "Stay away from anger and revenge. Keep envy far from you, for it only leads you into lies." I was dancing with anger and letting it pull me down. As I read these verses in the Bible, I realized I was being led into lies.

I repented for my anger and started to deal with it. I quieted my heart in the presence of God and asked myself, "Why am I so angry?" The answer was multi-dimensional and consisted of many layers of emotional pain. I am still unpacking the details, but the relief of seeing the truth that anger leads to lies helped me to have the strength to hand my pain over to God. This was a key part of my healing.

My grief became a gift because it allowed me to see my anger from a new perspective. I then chose to repent and step out of agreement with the lies. The truth was that I did not have to stay angry because I could face the root of my anger and my loss.

My loss did not define my life. On the contrary, it helped me to face my pain, and in facing it, I could give it to God. I realized that God wanted to reveal my issues to me. I no longer wanted to hide from them. I gave God permission to heal every part of my heart that was in pain. It is truly beautiful how God reaches in and redeems us.

Do you want God to reveal to you the issues you are facing? Will you allow Father God to use your grief to heal your soul?

**Reflection Questions**
Will you invite Father God to reveal the specific lies you may be believing, and ask him to open your eyes to what you cannot yet see?

In what areas of your life do you feel like you have "missed it" with God?

What are the lies in your heart that are leading you to anger, revenge, or envy?

**Declarations**
- I choose to quiet my heart before God and wait patiently for him.
- I declare I will stay away from anger, revenge, and envy.
- I trust God to reveal to me every lie I am believing. (This may take some time, but stay with it.)
- God opens my eyes and shows me the things I do not see.
- God's love defines me.

## Activation

Sit down with your journal and quiet your heart. Focus on the truth that Jesus is taking care of your every need. Imagine yourself in a beautiful tulip garden with Jesus. There are rows and rows of pink, red, white, purple, and yellow tulips. You are both sitting on a metal bench feeling the warmth of the sun taking in the breathtaking view of colorful tulips.

Ask Jesus to show you the things you do not see about your grief journey. Take a deep breath and write down each lie you are believing regarding your grief. Ask Jesus to reveal the things you don't see and to expose the lies you are believing, then write down his response.

## My Heart Today

## Prayer

*Father God,*

*Teach me how to quiet my heart in your presence and to wait patiently for you. I ask you to use my grief as a catalyst to heal my soul. Expose the lies in my heart that are leading me into anger, revenge, or envy. I repent for believing the lies that keep me bound. (Name each lie you have believed).*

*I choose to see your way over my way. I have suffered deep grief, and I invite you in to use my grief to heal my soul. I give you permission, Father God, to heal each and every place of pain in my heart.*

*In Jesus' name, I pray,*
*Amen*

# Day 7

## Becoming Humble of Heart

*"Just a little while longer and the ungodly will vanish; you will look for them in vain. But the humble of heart will inherit every promise and enjoy abundant peace."*
*Psalm 37:10-11*

In my grief process, it hit me that the humble of heart are the ones who will inherit every promise and enjoy abundant peace. Which brings us to the question: What truly is humility?

Merriam-Webster dictionary defines humility as "freedom from pride or arrogance."[1] Walking in pride and arrogance implies a belief system with the mindset that I can face my life in my own strength without the help of God.

Nothing has humbled me more than losing my husband to suicide. Without the strength of God, I could have never survived the deep level of trauma and loss. It has also forever changed how I interact with others.

I love how Psalm 37:10 says, "Just a little while longer and the ungodly will vanish; you will look for them in vain." My grief has given me a new perspective on many of my life's most significant questions. How does a loving God do away with the ungodly? We're all ungodly at some point in our lives. I always thought this verse meant that God would punish the ungodly people. But now I see it differently.

As we align our hearts with God's heart, we receive the grace to love those who have hurt us. It's not that the people actually vanish; it's just that their issues no longer bother us. After losing my husband to suicide, I have a new perspective on emotional pain. My empathy for others has increased, and with this deeper understanding, I see things I never noticed before. For example, when I see others acting cruel, callous, or uncaring, I now realize they are simply suffering emotionally. At some point in their lives, their hopes were crushed, which led them to become arrogant or negative or exhibit other undesirable traits.

The reason we're looking for the ungodly ones in vain is that our hearts have changed. We see others differently, and they no longer trigger our pain, so we do not perceive them in the same way. Instead of judging that person, a deep compassion now fills my heart for what they may have faced in this life. This kind of empathy allows us to pray for others and ask God to heal their pain.

## Reflection Questions
Where are you operating in pride and arrogance?

In which situations are you relying on your own strength instead of relying on God's strength?

Is there someone in your life that God wants you to pray for today?

## Declarations
- I am humble of heart.
- I inherit every promise of God.
- I enjoy abundant peace every day, no matter what I face.
- My empathy for others is increasing every day.

## Activation
Imagine yourself at the beach with your toes in the sand. Feel the warmth of the sun on your skin and look up at the sky. Take a deep breath and breathe in the salt air. Invite Jesus to change your perspective and humble your heart. Ask him to align your heart with his heart for people. Forgive those who have hurt you by naming each one and how they

offended you. Repent for holding an offense and ask Jesus to forgive you. Offer each person to Jesus and ask him to humble you and give you empathy for them.

## My Heart Today

## Prayer

*Holy Spirit,*

*Thank you for your comforting presence in my heart. I ask you to expose and lead me away from my own pride and arrogance. Thank you for humbling me to see your truth and to live my life according to your standard of love. Please show me who you would like for me to pray for today. I lift that person up to you and ask you to heal their emotional pain. Give me a humble heart so that I can inherit every one of your promises and enjoy abundant peace.*

*In Jesus' name, I pray,*
*Amen*

# Day 8

## *God's Forever Reward*

*"For the Lord takes care of all his forgiven ones while the strength of evil men will surely slip away. Day by day the Lord watches the good deeds of the godly, and he prepares for them his forever-reward."*
*Psalm 37:17-18*

I remember my husband Brett as a Jesus lover. He had a heart of gold, and he was a giver. Brett ministered God's love to whoever he met. It's very difficult for me to reconcile him taking his own life with him being a godly man. But the two actions coexist, leaving a confusing dichotomy. When I look at Psalm 37:18-19, it settles the issue by confirming to me that Brett is still loved and cared for by God.

Suicide and any other type of sudden loss open up a plethora of questions. Each path leads to either a lie or the truth. God did not stop caring for my husband, Brett, because he battled suicidal tendencies. Nor did God reject him because he chose suicide. I believe Brett is receiving the forever reward God prepared for him right now while he's in heaven.

One of the best changes of perspective that I have encountered in dealing with the suicide and sudden loss of my spouse is that I now know that he is in heaven. I had an encounter with Father God, asking him if Brett was with him. Then the most miraculous thing happened. God let me feel his love for Brett. After that, I knew Brett was in heaven with every fiber of my being.

Then I asked God if he was using nature to show me that he was still taking care of me, even though I lost my husband and felt so alone. I specifically asked about seeing butterflies and dragonflies because I had

39

been seeing them everywhere since Brett died. Was it a sign from God? The same day I asked the question, a butterfly flew directly into my chest. It hit my heart. I gasped, and instantly, I knew God was answering my question.

A short while later, my doorbell rang. I went to the front door and answered it. After stepping outside my house to chat with my neighbors, a dragonfly landed on my finger. It was double confirmation that these encounters with butterflies and dragonflies were signs from heaven, confirming God's love for me and the promise that I will be reunited in heaven with my husband, because he was a fellow believer.

Have you experienced confirmation from God that you are loved and taken care in your grief season? Before losing my husband, I would not have given much thought to these butterfly and dragonfly encounters. But the grief has slowed me down and opened my heart to receive God's love in new ways.

## Reflection Questions
What questions do you have for Jesus about your sudden loss?

How does it make you feel knowing that you have a forever reward waiting for you in heaven?

Do you feel taken care of by Jesus? Why or why not?

## Declarations
- Jesus loves me and takes care of me.
- Jesus prepares my forever reward for me.

## Activation
Sit down, take five deep breaths, and relax your body. Focus on the truth of this scripture, in Psalm 37:17-18, that God is taking care of you. Name three things you are grateful for and thank Jesus for them. Look at the questions you wrote down for Jesus from question #1. Ask him to speak to your heart about each question regarding your sudden loss. Write down his responses.

## My Heart Today

## Prayer

*Father God,*

*I thank you for taking care of all of me, your forgiven one, just as you promised in Psalm 37. I realize how much you have forgiven me for, and I thank you for this. I also thank you for preparing my forever reward and the forever rewards of my loved ones who believe. Thank you for seeing each of our hearts. You are a good God, and I thank you for taking care of me and my loved ones on both sides of heaven. Heal my heart of this grief, and please continue to give me your perspective on my life.*

*In Jesus' name, I pray,*
*Amen*

# Day 9

*God Provides More Than Enough*

*"Even in a time of disaster he will watch over them, and they will always have more than enough no matter what happens."*
*Psalm 37:19*

The words of Psalm 37:19 could not be more applicable in times of grief. My entire life changed when I learned that my husband had taken his own life, but my every need was still met. I was facing a personal disaster of enormous proportions. Yet even during this difficult time, I felt Jesus guiding me and offering me an incredible amount of grace. If I needed help with childcare for my toddler, someone would call and offer to babysit. When I worried about finances, I would get a call saying I was receiving a refund check for this or that. It was unbelievable.

In my early days of grief, I saw how God protected me from myself. My anger was overwhelming. I surprised myself with the depth of my emotions. The despair and shame were like a heavy coat on a hot, humid day. I wanted it off, and I felt like I could not breathe, but I didn't know what to do with it or where to put it. It felt like a recording was being spoken to my heart, asking myself over and over again: "How do I live with this horrible reality?"

Each morning, Jesus would lead me to read Psalm 37. Today, he reassured me that even in a time of disaster, he is with me. Do you feel Jesus with you in your disaster?

Sometimes all we need to know is that we're not alone. On this day, I didn't need Jesus to take away my pain. What I needed was the reassurance that he was there with me in it all. I was learning that I could rely on Jesus to show me the way and teach me how to fully embrace my new reality.

My grief was changing. I began to see the value in my grief, and I no longer wanted to run away from it; instead, I started to embrace it. My love-hate relationship with my grief was easing into a gentle knowing that this season was for me and not against me. I understood that Jesus was watching over me, and it started to dawn on me that I had a choice. Was I going to truly believe that my life was happening for me and not to me? Would I embrace my emotional pain and learn from it, or would I despise it?

I decided to embrace my grief and the waves of emotional pain because now I knew Jesus was there with me all along. He had never left my side. I couldn't do it alone, but with Jesus by my side, I decided I could face and eventually overcome this pain. My prayer for you is that with Jesus by your side, you can also start to face and then overcome your pain.

## Reflection Questions
When reflecting on times of disaster in your life, can you recall how God watched over you? Explain your answer.


Do you trust God to provide for all of your needs? Why or why not?


How is God providing for you today?


## Declarations
- Even in a time of disaster, God is watching over me.
- God cares for me gently and perfectly.
- I will always have more than enough, no matter what happens.

## Activation

Focus on the truth that even in a disaster, Jesus will watch over you. Begin by thanking Jesus for all the ways he has provided for you over the past three days. Even though your emotions may be spiraling, having breath in your lungs is one of the ways Jesus is providing for you. Write down each area of your life where you need to receive more than enough and decide to trust Jesus with each of these requests.

## My Heart Today

## Prayer

*Dear Jesus,*

*Thank you for watching over me and protecting me, even during times of disaster. I want to feel your presence by my side during this season of grief. I open my heart to you, Jesus, and ask you to let me experience your presence. No matter what life throws my way, you are always with me. I ask you to show me your grace in every part of my life.*

*Teach me how to have a grateful heart and trust you with my deepest fears and regrets. Make me an overcomer and fill me with your extravagant love. Partner with me to help me become who you intended me to be. I choose to believe your word that I will have more than enough, no matter what happens.*

*I pray this in Jesus' name,*
*Amen*

# Day 10

### God Lifts Us Up with His Hands

*"When YAHWEH delights in how you live your life, he establishes your every step. If they stumble badly they will still survive, for the Lord lifts them up with his hands."*
*Psalm 37:23-24*

I don't know about you, but my life is filled with mistakes. It's a good thing that this scripture reminds me that even if I stumble badly, I will still survive. The day my husband died, we were in a fight. We woke up that morning, and he was in a bad mood. I was aggravated and asked him why he couldn't ever wake up in a good mood.

We talked later that morning on the phone and got into another argument. My last words to him were something about us discussing it further later. But later never happened, and the guilt that arose from this conversation was borderline debilitating.

We were talking about what I would be fixing for dinner, and we were arguing. It all seemed so innocent. I hated that my reality involved me never talking to my husband face-to-face again. Like, why couldn't I have said "I love you" when I hung up that day? I never dreamed that we would not finish our conversation. I always said, "I love you," when we got off the phone or when he left the house.

Why would it happen that the one time I didn't say "I love you," I never saw him again? This reality tormented me. I beat myself up for this conversation for about four months straight, and then I got a revelation.

My husband was just as exasperated as I was because we couldn't find an answer. He was in physical pain, coming off of pain medication addiction, and dealing with the mental health issues of anxiety and depression. I wanted to help him, but I didn't know how. We reached a point where we both didn't know what to do, and we were aggravated with each other. Our fight was just us expressing our differences of opinion on how he would start to feel better.

I hate that my husband felt like the answer to our problems was suicide, but I can't take responsibility for his decision. At the end of the day, my husband decided to take his own life, and I had no say in that decision. The beauty of walking with Jesus is that he can renew and heal all things. Just as it says in Psalm 37:23, when God delights in how you live, he establishes your every step. God knew that my heart was not to hurt my husband that day.

My counselor asked me a question that helped me to forgive myself. She asked, "If he had come home that night, would you have regretted your conversation?" My answer was no because it was a valid conversation about our issues at the time. This realization brought me a sense of relief and set my heart at ease.

I decided to forgive myself and accept the truth that God delights in my life and guides every step I take. It's time to forgive yourself, too, because the Lord is lifting you up with his hands.

**Reflection Questions**
Do you have specific regret within the grief you are experiencing? Explain.


Can you forgive yourself for your part in the regret?


**Declarations**
- God delights in how I live my life, and he shows me where I need more grace.
- God establishes my every step.
  Even if I stumble badly, I will still survive.
- No matter what, God loves me, and he lifts me up with his hands.

## Activation

Write down the biggest regret you are experiencing and imagine Father God lifting you up over the situation. Just like an eagle, you are soaring high in the air above your problems as he empowers you. Forgive yourself for your part in the regret and receive God's forgiveness. Write down what Father God tells you about the situation.

## My Heart Today

## Prayer

*Holy Spirit,*

*I bring each of my regrets to you, and I ask you to redeem them. I regret when I (name each of your regrets). I forgive myself for how I acted and for what I said. Show me your perspective, Holy Spirit, and set me free.*

*Your word says in Psalm 37:24 that even if I stumble badly, I will still survive, for the Lord lifts me up with his hands. Thank you for lifting me up and out of my regrets. I repent for my actions, and I choose to receive your forgiveness. Teach me how to live a life that brings you delight. I ask you to establish every step of mine. I repent of my past regrets, and I ask that you forgive me and heal my heart.*

*In Jesus' name, I pray,*
*Amen*

# Day 11

###### Blessed to Become a Blessing

*"I was once inexperienced, but now I'm old. Not once have I found*
*a lover of God forsaken by him, nor have any of their children gone*
*hungry. Instead, I've found the godly ones to be the generous ones who*
*give freely to others. Their children are blessed and become a bless-*
*ing."*
*Psalm 37:25-26*

My husband and I have three children. I am the stepmom to our two sons, and we had our daughter about six years after getting married. My first thought when discovering my husband's death was regarding our three children. How could he leave them? They need their father. I thought to myself, "Maybe you are mad at me, but our children are the most precious gifts we could have ever received." I realize now that my husband's death had more to do with his mental state than our family, but at the time, I could not discern the difference between the two.

I was stunned by the situation. How would my children cope? What would our life look like moving forward? I immediately prayed for our children's hearts to be protected as they learned their father was no longer here on earth and processed what that would mean. Thoughts of how they would handle this swirled through my mind, leaving my heart unsettled and anxious.

For about a month, I read the entire chapter of Psalm 37 every day. Each time I reached verses 25-26, my heart would calm down. My husband may have forsaken our children, but God the Father would never abandon us. I began to accept the truth that we will survive my husband's suicide, and eventually, we will all thrive again.

Knowing that this verse says that lovers of God are never forsaken by him calms my heart. The truth is that God will see us through this trial, and he will see you through yours. We will not go without, but instead, we will be blessed to become a blessing. I have come to embrace this truth for myself and my three children, believing that experiencing the loss of my husband and their dad creates empathy for others. Because of our own pain, we can now offer support to friends and family who have also lost loved ones. With Jesus, our trials become our strengths.

My children are bouncing back from losing their dad faster than I expected. It is comforting to see them getting healed. We still have a long way to go, but I clearly see Jesus' hand at work in each of their lives. With God, we are never alone, and he takes care of our every need.

### Reflection Questions
Where do you feel forsaken or left alone?


Do you believe that God will heal these situations? Why or why not?


How are you practicing empathy for others given what you have experienced?


### Declarations
- God will never abandon me or forsake me.
- God provides for me and my family.
- I choose to be generous and give to others.
- I am blessed to become a blessing to others.

## Activation

Focus on the truth that God will never forsake you or abandon you. He will bless you to become a blessing. Read the scripture, Psalm 37:25-26, out loud. Take a deep breath and receive each of God's truths in this scripture. Write down the areas where you feel forsaken or abandoned. Ask Jesus to intervene in each place of pain and speak to you about his perspective on each situation.

Now write down all the areas where God has blessed you. Read your blessings aloud each morning for the next three mornings to remind you that God has not abandoned you, even if your reality looks different from what you thought it would be.

## My Heart Today

## Prayer

*Dear Jesus,*

*Thank you for never forsaking me or my family. You have generously provided for all our needs. Please heal our hearts from the sudden loss we never wanted. Touch our lives with your extravagant love. Help me and my family fulfill our God-given destiny. Teach me how to be a blessing to others.*

*In Jesus' name, I pray,*
*Amen*

# Day 12

## *God Never Deserts His Devoted Lovers*

*"If you truly want to dwell forever in God's presence, forsake evil and do what is right in his eyes. The Lord loves it when he sees us walking in his justice. He will never desert his devoted lovers; they will be kept forever in his faithful care, but the descendants of the wicked will be banished."*
*Psalm 37:27-28*

Suicide and sudden loss marred my life with their brutality. The cruel reality of my husband's choice to end his life knocked on my door each morning. I had to learn to forsake evil. To forsake means to renounce or turn away from entirely.[2]

I had to decide each morning not to allow my husband's death to negatively define my future. If I concentrated on his suicide instead of his character, I would be doomed. I chose to remember the good times and our love for one another. Eventually I had to forsake dwelling on my every mistake and blaming myself. However, the anger boiling up from his choice to willingly take his life was very difficult. As his wife, I found a great deal of betrayal and rejection in his decision.

Looking at my situation from God's eyes, I knew that the right thing to do was to fully forgive my husband. This was, to say the least, very difficult. I loved him with all my heart, but boy, I was mad!

I had to remind myself that forgiveness was not the same as agreement. I will never agree with my husband's decision to take his own life, but I do forgive him for doing it. By forgiving Brett and walking away from reliving his death in my mind over and over again each day, I was set free from torment and regret.

My husband would never want me to live in torment. The truth was that Brett loved all of us deeply. He would not want us to suffer. I slowly began to accept that my husband would want me to enjoy my life.

Psalm 37:28 says, "He will never desert his devoted lovers; they will be kept forever in his faithful care..." After reading verse 28 for several weeks, I came to understand on a deeper level that God the Father never deserts us. He faithfully cares for our every need. I kept thinking about all the times that God was faithful to us. There were so many memorial stones on which I could look back.

When you're faced with grief, it exposes your true belief system. At first, I felt deserted and abandoned. As the days and months progressed, I realized I was believing a lie. The truth was that Father God never deserts or abandons us, and my faith and trust are in him. I concluded that my husband knew our faith would carry us, and it has. What conclusion can you draw from your grief?

## Reflection Questions
What painful situation is knocking on your door each morning? Explain.

What do you believe about this situation? Name the thoughts running through your mind.

What are the truths (see Appendix A) that will turn you away from and renounce the negative thoughts and emotions surrounding this situation?

Who do you need to forgive and why?

## Declarations
- I will walk away from anger and renounce evil.
- I choose to be vulnerable and look at the root of my emotional pain.

- God will never desert me, because I am his devoted lover.
- I am kept forever in God's faithful care.

## Activation

Ponder the truth that you are kept forever in God's faithful care. Receive God's love as you dismantle the lies around the painful situation you are facing. Get some index cards or tear a piece of paper into smaller pieces. On one side, write the negative thoughts and emotions you're experiencing. On the other side, write God's truth and a scripture that contradicts the negative thought and emotion. Then, on another sheet of paper, make a list of the truths and scriptures. Start speaking them out loud over your life for the next 30 days.

## My Heart Today

## Prayer

*Father God,*

*Teach me how to dwell in your presence and help me forsake evil. Show me how to renew my mind with your truth each day. Reveal to me what and who I need to forgive. Set me free from torment and regret. I want to do what is right in your eyes. I accept the truth that you, my Heavenly Father, will never desert me, your devoted lover. I will be kept forever in your faithful care. Thank you for taking care of all my needs.*

*I pray this in Jesus' name,*
*Amen*

# Day 13

## Becoming A Faithful Lover of God

*"The faithful lovers of God will inherit the earth and enjoy every promise of God's care, dwelling in peace forever."*
*Psalm 37:29*

I want to be known as a faithful lover of God. As you can see in this scripture, there are many perks. I'm all about inheriting the earth, enjoying every promise of God's care, and dwelling in peace forever.

But what does it mean to be a faithful lover to him? I believe it involves walking in intimacy and vulnerability with Jesus. It looks like removing the protective walls around my heart and allowing myself to feel and work through my emotions. It means peeling away layers of self-protection to uncover my true beliefs. I cannot be a faithful lover of God if I am secretly operating in doubt and unbelief.

My grief revealed my layers of self-protection so deeply that I was repulsed by them. I recognized that I am a chronic people pleaser, always struggling to say no because I want to be liked. I felt unloved if I wasn't liked by everyone in the room. This flaw blocked me from reaching my divine destiny. After taking this to Jesus, I understood clearly that I needed to repent for my approval addiction, which had become an idol. I often went the extra mile for others at the expense of myself. Eventually, I realized that God's love is sufficient for me, and not everyone will like me. I let go of my need to be approved and embraced the truth that God's love is all I truly need.

The silver lining to my grief was that as my sin was exposed to me, I could hand it right over to Jesus, and he would heal my heart on the spot.

The more I became honest with myself, the easier it became to repent of my sin and renew my mind.

Grieving my husband also exposed this raw sense of wanting to live an authentic life. I now have this newfound appreciation for every milestone and gratitude for the little things. I realize that spending time together with loved ones is the best gift we can give each other.

I want to be a faithful lover to God because he was first a faithful lover to me. He loves me despite all my flaws, and he doesn't hold back his affection. My grief has given me the gift of slowing down and appreciating the small moments of life. Ironically, through my tears, my love of life has grown exponentially.

### Reflection Questions
What areas of your life cause you to doubt God will help you?

Where do you need to repent for operating in self-protection rather than relying on God?

What walls do you have up around your heart to protect yourself?

Can you look around and notice how your grief has positively transformed your life? Explain.

### Declarations
- I am a faithful lover of God.
- I choose to be vulnerable with Jesus.
- I will inherit the earth and enjoy every promise of God's care.
- I will live in peace forever with the Holy Spirit in my heart.

## Activation

Close your eyes and take a few deep breaths to relax. Think about being a faithful lover of God and dwelling in peace. Now, visualize one of the walls around your heart that hinders you from peace. Write down the negative beliefs and emotions that built this wall. Shut your eyes again and ask Jesus where he is and what he has to say about this wall. Work with him to renounce the negative beliefs, process the painful emotions, and forgive anyone who contributed to your pain. Then, write down what Jesus says to you about the situation. In your imagination, use a sledgehammer or axe to break down the wall. Grab Jesus' hand and walk over the rubble together into freedom. From now on, he is with you in this area of your life.

## My Heart Today

## Prayer

*Dear Jesus,*

*Thank you for loving me in a way that makes me want more of you each day. Your extravagant love grounds me and has made me who I am to-day. Teach me how to be your faithful lover. I want to enjoy your every promise, experience your loving ways, and dwell in your peace forever. I choose to be vulnerable with you, Jesus, and share my heart with you. Show me the things I do not see and take down all the walls around my heart. Thank you for using my grief as a window into a different per-spective on my life. I give you permission to transform me into who you created me to be.*

*In Jesus' name, I pray,*
*Amen*

# Day 14

🔥

## *Pushed to the Edge*

*"They pushed me right up to the edge, and I was ready to fall, but you helped me to triumph, and together we overcame them all. Lord, you are my true strength and my glory-song, my champion, my Savior!"*
*Psalm 118:13-14*

My favorite memories of my husband are when we laughed together. He knew me so well, and we would burst into belly laughs over the silliest things. About five days into our honeymoon cruise, I told him that I wished I had one more gift card to use at the spa.

Brett had left our room to get us some snacks, and then the hotel phone rang. I answered it, and this guy with an accent told me I had just won a $500 gift card to the spa. I was ecstatic! I even thought to myself, "Brett and I just talked about this. I can't wait to tell him!"

About 20 minutes later, Brett walked back into the room, and I told him I had just won a new spa gift card. He collapsed on the floor, cackling and laughing so hard, yelling, "I can't believe you fell for that!" I realized at that moment that it was him calling me with the accent, telling me I won the gift card. After being mad at him for tricking me, we ended up laughing so much. Then I said, "Does this mean I don't have another gift card to the spa?" and we laughed again.

The sudden loss of my spouse to suicide pushed me to the edge of what I thought I could handle. My sadness over not laughing with my husband again felt like too much to bear. Just like the scripture says, I was ready to fall. But as I kept reading, the promises of Jesus helping me to triumph and overcome it all deeply resonated within my heart. I also thought about how Brett would respond if I asked him for his opinion, and I know he would not want me to stay in my sadness.

I am encouraged by this verse because it gives me the promise that even when I'm ready to fall, Father God will help me to triumph and overcome it all. My season of facing sudden grief led me on a search for truth. That's why I love how the psalmist worships with these life-giving words, claiming that God is his true strength and his glory-song, his champion and savior.

The only way I can heal from this deep a loss is with Jesus. I have decided to open my heart and make Jesus my champion and savior over this grief and my future. Will you join me in trading in a broken heart for the strength and glory of God?

## Reflection Questions
What is pushing you to the edge in your life right now?


What areas of your life feel like they are falling apart?


How is Jesus helping you to triumph over your situation?


## Declarations
- No matter what I face, Jesus helps me to triumph and overcome it all.
- Jesus is my true strength, my champion, and my savior.

## Activation
Imagine yourself locking hands with Jesus and triumphing over all of your emotional pain. Run with him and feel the wind on your face. Now imagine that you sit down, and Jesus sits across from you. Write down the exact situation that makes you feel like you're at your breaking point. Close your eyes and hand the piece of paper to Jesus. Offer your situation as a sacrifice to him, then ask him to show you how he will help you triumph over your situation. Write down his response.

**My Heart Today**

**Prayer**

*Dear Jesus,*

*Thank you for your promise of helping me to triumph and overcome the crippling effects of grief. When sadness, loneliness, fear, and anxiety come knocking on my door, give me your strength to win the battle.*

*I choose you, Jesus, as my truth and my strength. May your glory run through my veins and be my catalyst against the pitfalls of despair. I choose to take you at your word and receive you as my champion and my savior. Will you trade in my soul pain for your victory? Please teach me how to reside in you and reclaim my life for your glory.*

*In Jesus' name, I pray,*
*Amen*

# Day 15

### God Lives in Me as Strength

*"But the Lord will be the Savior of all who love him. Even in their time
of trouble, God will live in them as strength."*
*Psalm 37:39*

I often think about the fight my husband and I had on the day he took
his life. It has been a very difficult fight to forgive myself for, and even
harder to stay in forgiveness. I often want to pick it up again and dissect
every word. I had resolved in my mind that without the fight, there's
no way Brett would have done it. But I know that's not true because I
believe he almost did it the week before.

As I was going over it again in my head, the Holy Spirit reminded me of
a time about one week before he died. Brett rolled over in bed early in
the morning and hugged me so tight that I ended up falling back asleep
in his arms. When I woke up, I looked in his eyes and said, "That was
nice. We need to do that more often." He didn't respond, which was
odd. I didn't think anything of it at the time, but looking back, I know
it was him telling me goodbye. I know this because when I looked up
his location on his phone that day, he was in the same location where he
committed suicide a week later.

Hindsight is 20/20, but I didn't know what I was looking for at the time.
Oh, how I wish we could have talked it out. I wish I could have reminded him once more of how much he was loved and cherished. I
would tell him that we could face anything together. I would say to him
how much I love him. But I also have to remind myself that this was
a choice he made on his own. As difficult as it is to fathom, it seems

as if it was a decision he had been thinking about for quite some time. That's why I felt deep encouragement when the Holy Spirit brought me to Psalm 37:39. The Holy Spirit reminded me that the Lord is my Savior. He saves me daily from beating myself up, and he forgives me. I love the promise in this verse. Even in my time of trouble, God will live in me as strength. It comforts me to know that I can rely on God for my strength because I certainly don't have it on my own. I can feel him holding me up as I face these tough days. What are you beating yourself up about? Let's give it to Jesus and forgive ourselves.

## Reflection Questions
How has the Lord saved you during your grief journey?


Is there a situation where you have forgiven yourself, then you pick it up again? Explain.


Will you decide today to forgive yourself once and for all?


How is God giving you strength in your grief season?


## Declarations
- Father God lives in me as strength.
- I am comforted by Holy Spirit.
- Even if I make a mistake, I am set free by Jesus.
- I choose to forgive myself and receive forgiveness from Jesus.

## Activation
Remember that the Holy Spirit lives in you as your strength and comforter. Ask the Holy Spirit to reveal the truth about your situation. Write down this truth. Now, take a deep breath, close your eyes, and imagine yourself standing in front of a small creek in the woods with Jesus. Although the water appears still, it is gently flowing in a soft current. Ask Jesus to show you how to keep moving forward even when it feels like everything is standing still. Forgive yourself and repent if you

believe you did anything wrong in the situation. Ask Jesus if you need to apologize to anyone to make things right. Decide to stop replaying the problem repeatedly in your mind and release it to Jesus. Ask him what perspective you might be missing or if you are deceived about anything. Write down his response.

## My Heart Today

## Prayer

*Dear Jesus,*

*I love you and I'm so thankful that you are my Savior. Thank you for saving me from myself and my thoughts. I repent of beating myself up over this situation. I forgive myself for (name the situation) and I receive your forgiveness. I ask you to help me stay in forgiveness toward myself and not pick up the situation again.*

*I choose to focus on you, Jesus, and your strength that lives in me. Without you, I could not face any of this pain. But with you by my side, I can look at anything. Allow me to see my situation as you see it. Please give me your eyes to see and your ears to hear. Change my perspective, Jesus, and set me free. I am so grateful that I can come to you in this vulnerable moment.*

*In Jesus' name, I pray,*
*Amen*

# Day 16

### Receiving Father God's Help

*"Because of their faith in him, their daily portion will be a Father's help and deliverance from evil. This is true for all who turn to hide themselves in him!"*
*Psalm 37:40*

My husband was a chronic pain patient due to the car wreck he suffered. I often went with him to the doctor. I can remember sitting in the waiting room area with him, feeling anxious about one of his upcoming surgeries, and my mind wandering to what I would do if he died.

I was reminded of this thought process recently while sitting alone and waiting for my doctor's appointment. When I thought about what I would do if my husband died, all I could say to myself was, "Well, now I know." But it was a gut-punch thought. I had to stop myself from ugly crying in public. Then I realized I had a choice in that moment: I could choose to remember the good times and be grateful for the time we shared, or I could remain stuck in the pain.

What I want to share with everyone reading this who is experiencing deep grief is this: Jesus is healing my heart, and he will heal yours as well. Grief is a process of emotional healing. We must acknowledge the pain and work through it, but by no means do we have to remain in that place forever. Yes, I cried and felt the emotions but the choice is in whether we stay there for days, weeks, or months at a time. The war is in our minds, and the battle is against negativity and lies. The truth is that our thoughts can either trap us or set us free. I have chosen the path of freedom, and I hope you will too.

The way to regulate the highs and lows of grief is to focus on the truth. Grief will inevitably bring unexpected moments of emotion and that is perfectly okay because it's part of the grieving process. I developed this response to my negative thoughts. When I have a debilitating thought that triggers major crying, I tell myself, "My life is happening for me and not to me. I am not a victim. I am an overcomer."

Once we learn to regulate our own emotions, we are no longer susceptible to the downward spiral of negativity. The first step to this regulation is identifying our thoughts and bringing them to truth. We can calmly choose to focus on the truth and receive God's love in our moments of emotional pain. I am not saying to avoid the pain, but rather to feel the pain while believing the truth.

During a grief season, many uncertainties arise. I handle them by examining my thoughts: Is this thought true? Does it align with the word of God? From there, I adjust and move forward. I encourage you to continue identifying your negative thoughts by writing them down. Once they are on paper, they lose their sting. Then, write the truth.

For example, if my negative thought is: "My life will never be happy again," I can write the opposite of that, which is: "My life is full of possibilities, and happiness is one of them." When I cry, I can say the truth to myself, which has a calming effect. I am honoring my emotions while believing the truth.

This is an ongoing process because our lives are like an onion, with many layers to peel back. Sometimes God heals an area of our lives and then asks us to revisit that area for deeper healing. I want to encourage you not to fall into the lie that you've already examined that thought or that Jesus has already healed that part of your heart. There is always room for more healing and personal growth. As we yield to the process, we receive our daily portion and deliverance from evil.

**Reflection Questions**
Where am I parked in my emotional pain?

In what areas of my life am I behaving like a victim?


What are some practical ways I can start moving toward healing again?


## Declarations
- My daily portion is help from Father God and deliverance from evil.
- I hide myself in Jesus and choose to trust him with my life.
- My life is happening for me and not to me.
- I am an overcomer.

## Activation
Your daily portion is a Father's help because of your faith in God. Imagine yourself on the side of a mountain looking over fields of colorful wildflowers. It's a cold day and you have a warm coat on your body. Breathe in the crisp mountain air and take in your surroundings. Look up to the sky and picture Father God descending from the clouds to stand next to you. Ask him to help you discern where you are getting stuck in your emotional pain. Write down your thought process and bring every lie to truth.

## My Heart Today

## Prayer

*Father God,*

*Because of my faith in you, my daily portion is your help and deliverance from evil. Psalm 37:40 says this is true for all who turn to hide themselves in him. I choose to hide myself in you, Father God. I ask you to deliver me from negative thoughts and a victim mentality. Teach me to discern a lie from your truth, even if I have already examined a particular lie. Help me to examine my thoughts. Show me how to take every thought captive and bring it to truth (2 Corinthians 10:5).*

*I choose to walk in your ways, Father God, and I surrender my life to you. I choose to believe that I have a bright future full of redemption, hope, and healing from Jesus. I agree with the truth that my life is happening for me and not to me. I receive your future for my life.*

*In Jesus' name, I pray,*
*Amen*

# Day 17

🔅

## Becoming Totally Dependent on God

*"What happiness comes to you when you feel your spiritual poverty!*
*For yours is the realm of heaven's kingdom. What delight comes to*
*you when you wait upon the Lord! For you will find what you long for.*
*What blessing comes to you when gentleness lives in you! For you will*
*inherit the earth."*
*Matthew 5:3-5*

During my deepest days of grief, I was looking for happiness around every corner. So, when I read this verse, it hit me differently than before. Why would happiness come to me when I felt my spiritual poverty?

Let's take a deeper look at the meaning of spiritual poverty in these verses. The Passion Translation footnote for the term "spiritual poverty" in Matthew 5:3 is, "Or, 'humble in spirit,' or, 'poor in spirit,' which means to be humble and totally dependent upon God for everything. It is synonymous with 'pious' or "saintly," not just in the sense of those who possess nothing. It could be translated "Delighted are those who have surrendered completely to God and trust only in him."[3]

My grief process has put me in a place of complete surrender to Father God. I realized early on that if I didn't trust him, I wouldn't make it through this season. My trust in him became emboldened in a new way because of my circumstances. It has most definitely humbled me and forced me into a new perspective of Jesus and his love.

According to Matthew 5:3-5, the blessings attached to being humble and surrendering your life to Jesus are happiness, finding what you long for, and inheriting the earth. It's so inspiring to me to think about how Jesus blesses our obedience so extravagantly, even when that obedience happens from a life circumstance you could never have imagined.

In my worst season, Jesus is bringing out the best for my life. That is humbling in itself. As I'm learning to trust on a deeper level, Jesus is releasing happiness and showing me a path to my deepest desires. My role is to receive his love in this new way. Again, it is so humbling to realize how incredibly loved I am despite the agonizing fear and anger arising from my grief.

Losing my husband has made me more dependent on God. I would have told you that I was fully surrendered to Jesus before Brett's death, but now it's different because I can no longer rely on my husband. Losing him made me realize that I had made my husband an idol or a false refuge in my life. I relied on my husband first for my well-being when I should have put God in this position. As soon as I realized this codependency, I repented and decided to change my thinking.

My new mindset is to stop relying on my circumstances to take care of me and instead accept that I will now prioritize Jesus and his power over my life, no matter what I face. I now fully realize that I can't control everything. After much thought, I choose to believe that the things beyond my control are safe because I can trust Jesus with every situation and circumstance.

As I depend more on Jesus, I am receiving more peace. I also am waiting on God for my future, and it's proving to be a wonderful experience. I want to encourage you to become more dependent on God and I believe you will watch your life change in the most beautiful ways.

**Reflection Questions**

Where have you relied on your circumstances or another person to sustain you instead of relying on Jesus?

Which circumstances do you want to surrender to Jesus and ask him to change?

How can you begin trusting Jesus more in your life?

## Declarations
- I will wait upon the Lord and find what I long for.
- Gentleness and happiness live in me.
- The things beyond my control are safe because I can trust Jesus with every situation and circumstance in my life.
- I am totally dependent on God for everything in my life.

## Activation
Imagine yourself in your kitchen washing dishes at the sink. Jesus walks up and asks where the towels are because he's going to start drying the dishes. You feel surprised because it's unusual for Jesus to do such a mundane task like drying dishes. But, you hand him the towel anyway, and since you have his full attention, you ask him about the times when you've relied on others or circumstances to avoid trusting him. After discussing it, write down the people and circumstances you will now surrender to Jesus.

## My Heart Today

## Prayer

*Dear Jesus,*

*Thank you for being there for me when I needed you most. I'm asking you to continue to make me humble and utterly dependent on you because I know I can trust you no matter what I face in life. My feelings do not indicate the truth. They only reflect my belief system. You are the truth in my life. Change my belief system to line up with your truth.*

*Thank you for showing me your ways. I repent for the areas of my life where I have placed (name it) as an idol, trusting him/her/circumstance to take care of me and give me purpose instead of you. Will you forgive me?*

*I choose to believe now that you are all I need in this life. I choose to trust you. Thank you that when I decide to wait on you, Lord, I will receive what I long for. I love you, Jesus, and I want to become totally dependent on you.*

*In Jesus' name, I pray,*
*Amen*

# Day 18

🔥

## Opening My Eyes to See More of God

*"How enriched you are when you crave \*righteousness (\*or good-ness or justice)! For you will be satisfied. How blessed you are when you demonstrate \*tender mercy (\*or merciful to forgive)! For tender mercy will be demonstrated to you. What bliss you experience when your heart is pure! For then your eyes will open to see more and more of God."*
*Matthew 5:6-8*

In 2024, before my husband Brett passed away, I received a prophetic word. In part, it said, "Rayna, come close! Sit with me. Get to know me. I am drawing you into true friendship. Let us laugh together, mourn together, partner together…"

It was a beautiful invitation from God to come closer to him. I remember the first time I read it, and the word "mourn" really stuck out to me. I thought to myself, "I sure am glad I'm not mourning anything." Then here I am months later, mourning the death of my husband. I never would have dreamed I would be a widow!

It's such a shocking feeling to be married one day and not have a husband the next. Now, when I pick up the card with the prophetic word on it, the word "mourn" has an entirely new meaning. What struck me is that Father God wanted to mourn with me. I had never considered it until this moment. It was his tender mercy being demonstrated to me.

God is also mourning Brett's life because of all that was lost and all that could have been. It hit me that God's feelings were similar to what I had been experiencing. Every morning, I woke up and faced this insurmountable loss, and I am now realizing that Father God understands and feels it too. He had great plans for Brett on this earth, and it saddens him that Brett's destiny was not fulfilled.

I now feel his tender mercy, and my eyes are open to see more and more of God. I started to mourn with God and share my emotional pain with him. We cried together and laughed together. This revelation changed my perspective on how God views death. I don't know exactly what I thought about it before losing my husband, but now that I deeply understand grief with all of its uncertainties, I believe that God grieves too. The torment I feel grieves God just as it grieves me. This revelation makes me feel seen by God and has opened my eyes to see more of him.

Have you ever considered that God is grieving with you? I believe he wants to show you more of him so he can deeply heal your heart and bring you into your next season.

**Reflection Questions**

What words or concepts now have a different meaning to you because of your grief journey?

Did you ever consider that God is grieving with you? How does this revelation change your perspective?

How has Jesus shown you tender mercy in your grief journey?

**Declarations**
- I receive God's tender mercy.
- I crave righteousness, goodness, and godly justice.
- My eyes are open to see more of God.
- I forgive those who have hurt me, and I am satisfied.
- I experience bliss because my heart is pure.

## Activation

In this season of my life, I was concerned that I would never again wake up without being tormented by my husband's suicide. Tell Father God about the things that torment you and ask him his opinion. Forgive those who have hurt you and begin to process your pain with Father God. Let him mourn with you. Picture him crying next to you, hugging you, and talk to him about your pain. There is healing in crying and talking it out, especially when you're talking to Father God. Write down what you experience.

## My Heart Today

## Prayer

*Father God,*

*Thank you for showing me you are grieving with me. I feel comforted to know I am not alone in my feelings of loss and the sadness of what could have been. I will continue to share my innermost thoughts and sad feelings that torment me.*

*Thank you for showing me tender mercy while I mourn. I will now extend that same mercy to others. Thank you for giving me a pure heart. I ask you to open my eyes to see more and more of you, Father God.*

*In Jesus' name, I pray,*
*Amen*

# Day 19

⚜

## *Experiencing the Realm of Heaven's Kingdom*

*"How joyful you are when you make peace! For then you will be recognized as a true child of God. How enriched you are when persecuted for doing what is right! For then you experience the realm of heaven's kingdom."*
*Matthew 5:9-10*

In the initial weeks after my husband's funeral, I experienced many emotional ups and downs. In my grief, I started to blame others for how they were responding to the loss of my husband. For instance, someone posted on social media about Brett saying, "Social media is not always what it seems." This sentence tormented me. I started to blame myself for not seeing my husband's suicide coming. Then I was mad at myself for sharing our lives on social media because I felt judged and rejected.

None of these feelings genuinely reflected the situation. The person who wrote this post was truly grieving and expressed kind words. My subconscious belief that my husband's suicide was my fault was being triggered. A trigger is a natural trauma response that occurs when something in the present moment reminds your brain of a past trauma. As a result, your body reacts just like it did during the original experience, creating a familiar, yet sometimes overwhelming, response.

My reaction was to feel overwhelming torment and guilt. I needed to confront my belief that my husband's death was my fault and recognize it as the lie it was. Then, I could focus on the truth that my husband's death was a choice he made and not my fault. The issue was within my heart, not in the social media posts of people who loved us. I finally got the revelation that everyone around me was processing the shock of Brett's death just as much as I was. In their process, they were posting to social media to create awareness about suicide and its devastating effects. By taking a breather and looking at the situation from a different angle, I realized that my perception was skewed by my trigger of believing everything was my fault.

Matthew 5:9 says we receive joy when we make peace. I decided to make peace and forgive that person. I chose to look at the truth of the situation, which was that I was feeling guilty because I was wrongfully blaming myself. I also forgave myself. As soon as I did these things, my joy returned. I discovered that anger and blame towards others could not bring my husband back. They were only slowing me down in my healing journey.

## Reflection Questions
Is there someone in your grief journey who is triggering you? Explain.

Are you willing to forgive them? Remember, forgiveness is not reconciliation, and it's not saying they were right. It is handing them over to Jesus so he can handle them.

What new revelation is Jesus teaching you about your situation?

## Declarations
- I am joyful when I make peace.
- I choose to forgive others no matter what because forgiveness is not saying they are right, but handing the offense over to Jesus so he can judge the situation.
- I choose to look at truth no matter how painful it may feel.

## Activation
Imagine yourself sitting on your sofa with Jesus sitting next to you. You both are curled up with blankets on each side of the sofa. Look at him and ask him to show you what is triggering you in your grief journey. Then, look for the lies you are believing that surround this particular trigger. Write down each lie and then write down the truth that Jesus

shows you, counteracting the lie. Forgive anyone that Jesus highlights to you. Picture yourself handing this person over to Jesus. Write down what you experience.

## My Heart Today

## Prayer

*Holy Spirit,*

*You are my comfort in times of trouble. I ask you to show me the lies I am believing about others as I process my grief. Please show me where I am triggered and where I need to make peace with others. I choose to forgive and put them in your hands, even if I don't understand their behavior. I ask you to bring back my joy and help me experience the realm of heaven's kingdom. I want your perspective, Holy Spirit. Will you show me the way and help me? Please open my eyes to see and my ears to hear you and your direction for my life.*

*In Jesus' name, I pray,*
*Amen*

# Day 20

### Shining Brightly with God's Light

*"Your lives light up the world. For how can you hide a city that stands on a hilltop? And who would light a lamp and then hide it in an obscure place? Instead, it's placed where everyone in the house can benefit from its light. So don't hide your light! Let it shine brightly before others, so that your commendable works will shine as light upon them, and then they will give their praise to your Father in heaven."*
*Matthew 5:14-16*

About six months into my grief, I turned a corner. I started to believe deep in my heart that Brett would want me to be happy in my new life. I thought about his beautiful heart and all the times he said, "If anything happens to me, I want you to rejoice that I'm in heaven and that I am no longer in constant pain."

I also reminisced about how we discussed that if one of us died, the other should move on and remarry. We both agreed that the new spouse would have to love all of our children. But other than that, we never put any stipulations on it. It was as if we knew the other would make the right choice, because we agreed on what was best for our family.

I can feel the eyes of our community on my life as "the woman whose husband committed suicide." At first, it felt like a burden, but now it feels like redemption. No matter what we face in life, Jesus can heal us and set our hearts free. I think about this scripture, Matthew 5:14-16, and how our light has the ability to shine brightly to others. I have a choice in this moment to either shine brightly with God's light or succumb to the emotional pain.

I know Brett would not have taken his own life if he wasn't convinced it was the best thing for his family. Of course, I passionately disagree with his decision, but it was his choice, nonetheless. Here I sit having to deal with the consequences of his fatal decision. As I do, my heart is revived each morning by focusing intently on the belief that Father God deeply loves me. No matter what you are facing on your grief journey, you are also deeply loved by Father God. No circumstance you face will ever change this truth.

Matthew 5:16 says that we should not hide our light. The footnote for "light" in verse 16 is, "The Aramaic word for 'light' (noohra) is often used as a metaphor for teachings that bring enlightenment and revelation into the hearts of men. Light can also represent the presence of God ("the light of his countenance"). Jesus is the light of God within us."[4]

I believe I've turned a corner after receiving teachings from the Bible about Father God's love and the revelation that my life is not over. The Holy Spirit still lives in me, comforting me each time I need it, and that gives me hope for my future. Of course, my future is forever different, and there's a lot of pain to deal with because of that, but I now want God's light to shine in me again.

I want to reach others in pain and tell them that Father God is going to heal their hearts, too. I want you to know there's hope, no matter how bad it gets. You are walking through grief, not parking in grief. Let the gift of grief have its work in you, and then you will arise as a light on a hill.

The footnote for "commendable works" mentioned in verse 16 states, "Light and works are intertwined. We need the light of Christ in order to do good works. Our good works are like light shining upon their hearts."[5]

I started writing this devotional for my heart, and it has turned out that the process of writing about my grief and receiving Jesus' light has intertwined with the revelation that my grief has become a gift. Experiencing my deep emotions and learning from them has put me on a new path where I'm gaining a new layer of God's revelation and his light. His light is motivating me to do good works.

By the grace of God, I am starting to accept my new life as a widow with a future, and in that decision, there is a release of God's light. I believe God is releasing his light and his revelation into your life as well, and it will produce good works.

## Reflection Questions

What are some steps you can take to begin accepting your new life?

How can your story help others?

What are some ways that your life can be a light to the world? (For example, volunteer at church or at a local charity).

## Declarations
- My life lights up the world.
- My life leads others to Jesus.
- I am receiving more and more of Jesus' light every day.
- I produce commendable works.

## Activation

How has your grief dimmed your light? Write down the negative emotions you feel and how they are affecting your day-to-day life. Use Appendix A to find the counteractive positive emotion and declare it over your life. For example, I am no longer lonely because I belong, and I pursue connection with others. If this is not yet true in your life and you are dealing with loneliness, start by visiting some local churches. Finding a church family is a great way to experience connection with others.

## My Heart Today

## Prayer

*Father God,*

*I ask you to continue to show me your light in all things. Help me accept my grief and learn from it. Thank you for changing my perspective about scripture and your intentions for me. Knowing I'm extravagantly loved by you, Father God, has been my greatest gain in my grief.*

*I receive your love for me despite my extreme lack of understanding about why this happened to me. I choose to have unanswered questions and still trust you. I give you permission to show me more of you. Let your light shine in me and use my story for your good, Lord. I trust you in this new way, and I thank you for holding my hand through it all.*

*In Jesus' name, I pray,*
*Amen*

# Day 21

### Receiving God's Marvelous Love

*"For this reason the Lord is still waiting to show his favor to you so he can show you his marvelous love. He waits to be gracious to you. He sits on his throne ready to show mercy to you. For YAHWEH is the Lord of justice, faithful to keep his promises. Overwhelmed with bliss are all who will entwine their hearts in him, waiting for him to help them. Yes, the people of Zion who live in Jerusalem will weep no more. How compassionate he will be when he hears your cries for help! He will answer you when he hears your voice!"*
*Isaiah 30:18-19*

When I read Isaiah 30:18-19, my first thought is that I missed it. I wanted God to be gracious to heal my husband. I wanted favor to fall upon the new business my husband and I had just started. But then the reality hit me that my circumstance of being a widow was my husband's choice.

So, here I am sitting alone with all of my unanswered prayers and holding the bag. I still have to get the kids to school and cook dinners. The bills need to be paid, and the grass needs to be cut. By God's immeasurable grace, Brett went to heaven. However, I am left to deal with the repercussions of his sudden departure. Yet again, I realize that I have to change my perspective.

The Lord is waiting to show his favor to me so he can show me his marvelous love. Losing my husband to suicide feels like anything but love. But even in my anger and feelings of betrayal and loss, Father God waits to be gracious to me. He wants to show me mercy.

In my pain, I decided to relinquish my negative emotions and to receive God's mercy and grace. At this moment, when I started to receive the truth from God, my heart began to fill with peace. I experienced the bliss that's referenced in verse 18, and it is intriguing to me.

I want this feeling of peace to stay. I want to entwine myself with Father God. I finally feel like I can handle being a single mom and all the curveballs being thrown my way. I want to stay in this place because the despair of the past few months has been awful.

In verse 19, it says that we will weep no more. I have decided to take Father God at his word. I choose to believe that he will be compassionate when he hears my cries for help. He will answer me when he hears my voice. This encourages me to keep praying and keep reaching out to him with all my desires and needs. I encourage you to do the same.

Ever since my husband died, I can tangibly feel God's presence. I believe this is another aspect of the gift of grief. I never want his presence to leave, and I believe that keeping my life entwined with Jesus is the key to staying in this place of intimacy.

**Reflection Questions**
What negative emotions do you need to release so you can feel overwhelmed with bliss? You can use Appendix A for guidance.

What are some ways you can cultivate peace in your life?

Is there a new boundary you need to set? Explain.

What is your most prominent prayer request right now?

**Declarations**
- I open my heart to receive Father God's marvelous love.
- I will release my negative emotions to the Holy Spirit.
- Father God is the Lord of justice and he keeps his promises to me.

- I entwine my heart with Jesus while waiting for him to help me overcome my grief.
- I cry out to the Holy Spirit for help, and he comforts me.

## Activation

Close your eyes and imagine Jesus sitting beside you on a porch swing on a summer day. Swing with him back and forth, feeling the slight breeze blowing through the air. Receive his marvelous love. Share your most urgent prayer request with Jesus. Ask him to give you the faith to believe that he will answer. Talk to Jesus about your request. Is there anyone you need to forgive? Forgive yourself if necessary. Are you harboring negative beliefs about the outcome? Do you feel fearful or doubtful? Where did that fear originate? Hand all the "what ifs" over to Jesus as you continue swinging with him on the porch. Ask him what he has to say about your situation. Write down his response.

## My Heart Today

## Prayer

*Father God,*

*Show me how to continue to entwine my heart with yours. I want to hear your voice and see you in everything. You are the God of justice, and you're faithful to keep your promises. I need your help with (name your most prominent prayer request).*
*Overwhelm me with your bliss as I wait for you to help me. I want to reach a point where I no longer weep.*

*I cry out to you, Father God, for your help, and I ask for your compassion to fall on my life. I know you will answer me. I choose to look for you in every situation and around every corner. I love you, Father God, and I am so thankful that I can come to you like this. Fill my heart with your hope and your marvelous love.*

*In Jesus' name, I pray,*
*Amen*

# Day 22

⁂

## *My Hope Is in God Alone*

*"And now, God, I'm left with one conclusion: my only hope is to hope in you alone!"*
*Psalm 39:7*

Intimacy has been explained to me by my grief counselor as "into me you see." Jesus sees everything in my heart and he still loves me. Just as it says in Psalm 39:7, I am left with the conclusion that my only hope is in Jesus.

Grief tore through my heart like an axe splitting firewood. One minute, I was managing daily life fine, and the next, my heart felt shattered. On one hand, I missed my husband and mourned all that might have been. I felt such compassion for him, even pity. But then, on the other hand, I was furious. Deep anger surged within me. Thoughts like, "Why couldn't he choose us? How could he do this to our children? What in the hell was he thinking?" kept rushing through my mind.

I was also dealing with overwhelming loneliness. My life partner had left the world and I felt very vulnerable. I had so many questions that seemed never to be answered. I kept getting angry as deep emotions rose to the surface of my heart. I chose to go past the anger and ask myself what I truly was feeling. The terrible feelings of betrayal and abandonment started rising to the surface.

After talking to many people about suicide, I learned that the person doing it rarely considers others. They are in so much pain themselves that they can only see their pain. Learning that my husband probably did not consider me and the kids was both a relief and a setback. I also think my husband believed the lie that we were better off without him. Because of that lie, he pulled the trigger, and our lives changed forever.

I can either live in the delusion that my husband was perfect, and on the flip side, believe the lies of the enemy to stay angry and betrayed, or I can choose the truth. It's so easy to get entangled in the lies. That's where staying connected to Jesus is so important. Like Psalm 39:7 says, "my only hope is to hope in [God] alone." As I continued to surrender my emotions to the Lord, he kept leading me to the truth, no matter how severe my negative emotions became.

I believe the truth is that my husband encountered the perfect storm of terrible circumstances, and he made a horrible mistake. A mistake that is final and cannot be changed on this side of heaven. But I will not allow Brett's mistake to drive my future. The truth is that Jesus never betrayed or abandoned me. I can continue to place my hope in Jesus and he won't let me down.

I believe that if my husband could come back, he would tell me that he made a mistake. Since that is not a possibility right now, I choose to believe what Jesus is telling me. My husband's suicide was not my fault. Though I may feel alone, I am not. I am surrounded by an incredible support system and Jesus is meeting my every need. He will do the same for you. Open your heart to receive his love in a new way. Surrender your grief as a sacrifice to Jesus.

Ever since surrendering my grief to Jesus, my life has been getting better, and my heart is healing. I choose to place my hope in Jesus, and I now have reassurance from him that my children will thrive and fulfill their God-given destinies because that's his promise to me. I will keep letting Jesus in and asking him the hard questions. I invite you to join me in this and release the pent-up pain in your heart.

We can trust Jesus to speak to our hearts with the words we need to hear each morning to get us through the day.

## Reflection Questions

What's your most difficult question for God right now? (I encourage you to ask "what" and not "why" because sometimes the "why" questions can cause us to run in circles).

What negative emotions are you surrendering to Jesus right now?

What mistakes are you holding yourself responsible for that you need to turn over to Jesus?

Are you willing to forgive yourself?

## Declarations

- I have intimacy with Jesus, and I am allowing him to see the deepest pain in my heart.
- I open my heart to receive hope from Jesus for my situation.
- I choose hope instead of despair.

## Activation

Play a worship song and sing to the Lord. After the worship song, take three deep breaths and relax in God's presence. Ask God your most difficult question from the above reflection questions. Sit in his presence and be open to perceive his response. He may remind you of a scripture, or you may have a childhood memory. Whatever happens in this space, honor it and pursue it with Father God. Write down what you perceive.

## My Heart Today

## Prayer

*Dear Jesus,*

*I want to have intimacy with you. I give you permission to see the intimate places of my heart where I share my deepest thoughts and contemplations. Lead my heart to your truth. Please help me to discern your will for my past, present, and future. I place my hope and my life in your hands, for I have reached the conclusion that my only hope is to hope in you alone. I am forever yours.*

*In Jesus' name, I pray,*
*Amen*

# Day 23

I Am Watered and Protected by God

*"I, the Lord, watch over my vineyard of delight. Moment by moment, I water it in love and protect it day and night. There is no anger in me, for if I found briars and thorns I would burn them up and march to battle against them. So let the branches cling to my protection when they make true peace with me. Yes, let them make me their friend."*
*Isaiah 27:3-5*

My grief journey has emerged from despair to deep friendship with the Lord. Oddly enough, I was not mad at Jesus when I discovered my husband's lifeless body in his car that dreadful afternoon. When I lost my husband, it solidified my relationship with Jesus. It confirmed to me that everything in this life is temporary except for Jesus.

I clung to Jesus for my protection. I love how verse 3 of Isaiah 27 says that the Lord waters me in love and protects me day and night. As I pictured him watering me with a hose and protecting me from invaders, Jesus gently showed me that I was blaming myself for Brett's death. I didn't blame God; I blamed myself.

Here I am facing my worst tragedy, and my coping mechanism is to blame myself. It's the same thing that children of divorced parents do to themselves. As absurd as it is to believe someone else's choice is my own fault, I believed it, and I had to break away from it.

These thoughts were the briars and thorns in my heart that kept hurting me. They were lies tormenting me and keeping me away from true heart healing.

In verse 4, the Lord says that he will burn up these briars and thorns and march to battle against them. I love this. Jesus is marching into battle and fighting for me when I can't fight for myself. It's his protection over me to show me the truth and lead me away from the lie.

I repented for believing the lie that it was my fault my husband committed suicide, and I chose to believe the truth that Brett's death was beyond my control. What false beliefs are you holding about your grief? Allow Jesus to correct your wrong thinking and guide you toward healing.

## Reflection Questions
What are you angry about in your grief journey?


Where is anger masking your true emotions?


What is the true emotion? Refer to Appendix A.


What lies are you believing about your circumstance?


Are you blaming yourself for something that is not your fault? Explain.



## Declarations
- I cannot control everything, but I can trust God with it all.
- Like a gardener waters and protects his garden, Jesus waters and protects me.
- My anger is burned up as Jesus marches to battle against it.
- I choose to let my true emotions surface.

## Activation
Imagine yourself standing next to Jesus as he is watering his vineyard. He has built a metal fence around the vineyard, protecting it from invasive animals. Jesus looks over to you and says, "This vineyard is the garden of your heart." You are being watered and protected by Jesus. Ask Jesus to show you what briars and thorns are in your garden.

Where are you angry? What negative emotions are surfacing? What lies are you believing? Write down the answers to each of these questions, then hand them over to Jesus to burn up. Imagine him marching to battle against each one as he meticulously prunes the garden of your heart.

## My Heart Today

## Prayer

*Dear Jesus,*

*I am part of your vineyard, and you watch over my life with delight. Thank you for watering me with love and protecting me day and night. Even on my worst days, you care for me, and I can feel it.*

*Burn up the briars and thorns in my heart that are tormenting me. Show me the lies I am believing and bring each one to truth. Make me tender again, trusting you with everything I have. I cling to your protection because I choose to make true peace with you. Will you make me your friend? I love you, Jesus, and I want to be close to you.*

*In Jesus' name, I pray,*
*Amen*

# Day 24

☂

## *Embracing the Truth*

*"Jesus said to those Jews who believed in him, 'When you continue to embrace all that I teach, you prove that you are my true followers. For if you embrace the truth, it will release true freedom into your lives.'"*
*John 8:31-32*

I am learning through the experience of my grief that the teachings of Jesus are releasing freedom into my life. I have always been familiar with these scriptures, but I now have a different understanding.

In The Passion Translation by Dr. Brian Simmons, the footnote for verse 32 states, "The truth Jesus gives us releases us from the bondage of our past, the bondage of our sins, and the bondage of religion. Jesus was speaking these words to those who were not fully free from man's traditions. Truth must be embraced and worked out through the divine process of spiritual maturity. The Greek word for 'truth' is reality. To embrace the reality of Christ brings more freedom into your life. See the book of Galatians for a clear explanation of the freedom Jesus refers to here."[6]

Losing my husband to suicide opened the door for me to embrace God's truth and begin the process of spiritual maturity. If the word "truth" in these verses means reality, then I have to ask, "What is my reality?"

I have chosen to believe in Jesus as my reality instead of the lies swirling in my mind and tormenting me over every word I spoke to my husband. I can't undo anything I said or didn't say. Oh, how I wish I had gotten to say, "I love you," just one more time. But my reality is that I didn't get that chance.

I had no idea that day was my last day with my precious husband. I must give myself grace in it all. If this same situation happened to someone I love, I would tell them to forgive themself. I have to take my own advice and apply it to my life.

I choose to forgive my husband for leaving us by taking his own life. I forgive myself for the embarrassment and shame of not knowing he would commit suicide. I receive Jesus' love for me in my toughest moments, and I look to him for my answers.

## Reflection Questions

If someone else experienced the same grief you're experiencing, what advice would you give them?

What do you need to forgive yourself for?

Who do you need to forgive? If you have already forgiven this person, humble yourself and forgive them again, and let your heart feel the release.

Do you find that you are looking to Jesus for your answers or to yourself? Explain.

## Declarations
- I am growing more spiritually mature each day.
- I submit to the divine process of spiritual maturity.
- I choose to be Christ's true follower and learn his truth every day.
- I embrace the truth of Yeshua (Jesus), and his truth releases true freedom into my life.

## Activation

Imagine yourself with Jesus in a stable of horses. You are walking with him past each stall, feeding the horses carrots, and petting their heads. As you see him care for the horses, imagine how much he cares for you. Ask him any questions you have about the new reality (truth) you are embracing during your grief season. Write down the answers you perceive.

## My Heart Today

## Prayer

*Dear Jesus,*

*I choose to embrace all that you teach. I look to you for answers to my many questions. Give me a deeper revelation of who you are and how to live my life according to your will. Encourage me with the future you have planned for me. Bring back my dreams and spark life into my passions, my dreams, and my future.*

*I ask you to guide me toward spiritual maturity so I can see my life from your perspective. Please show me where I need to forgive myself and others. Teach me how to accept my truth, my new reality, and bring more freedom into my life. I know you love me, and I trust in your love. I receive your love, and I love you too.*

*In Jesus' name, I pray,*
*Amen*

# Day 25

## *Remaining in Life-Union with Jesus*

*"I am a true sprouting vine, and the farmer who tends the vine is my Father. He cares for the branches connected to me by lifting and propping up the fruitless branches and pruning every fruitful branch to yield a greater harvest. The words I have spoken over you have already cleansed you. So you must remain in life-union with me, for I remain in life-union with you. For as a branch severed from the vine will not bear fruit, so your life will be fruitless unless you live your life intimately joined to mine."*
*John 15:1-4*

When my husband's mortality confronted me that difficult day, the truth of Jesus' love emerged from my heart. Nothing has made me closer to Jesus than losing my husband to suicide. I know that sounds crazy because I would have thought that I would blame the Lord for my loss and run away from him. But that didn't happen.

Going through my grief journey has fortified my life-union with Jesus. I knew deep down that the only way I could survive my husband's death was by staying connected with Jesus. It wasn't just a feeling; it was a knowing. I felt as if God had placed this truth in me many years ago for this very moment. He knew what I would face, and he prepared me for it.

I think of the analogy of a tea bag being dropped into boiling water. Whatever is inside that tea bag will be released by the hot water. My true belief system surfaced that day when my husband died—seeing his lifeless body awakened a newfound trust in Jesus within me. This trust is part of the gift I have received from my grief journey. But the trust did not start immediately.

At first, I realized how much I doubted Jesus' love for me. I had to ask myself why, and the answer was because everyone close to me (my parents, men I dated) always deserted me, just like Brett did with his suicide. I knew Jesus was the only one who could heal my heart from this terrible pain of rejection and abandonment. He was also the only one who could understand it at my level. Jesus has been with me my whole life, and he knew my unhealthy patterns and understood the depth of pain erupting in my heart.

Despite it all, I am encouraged by John 15:1-4 because the passage reminds me that the pruning brings a greater harvest. Deep in my spirit, I understood that I could not survive this pain without remaining in life-union with Jesus. Grief made me genuinely ready for him to trim away the parts of my life that were contributing to my heart pain.

I repented for doubting Jesus' love for me and invited him in to heal my emotional pain. We went on a journey, forgiving Brett, my parents, and the men I dated for rejecting and abandoning me. I forgave myself for engaging in the same unhealthy patterns for years and for abandoning myself.

In facing my tragedy, I also had to face all of the leftover thinking patterns and bad belief systems that I entertained day after day. These were from a life of believing lies and not knowing my true identity in Christ.

I decided to put my faith and hope in Jesus and learn what he had to say about me. I love how verse 3 says that the words God has spoken over us have already cleansed us. In the activation, let Jesus' words cleanse you. It is comforting to know that the fruit of my life is achieved when I grow closer to him. All we have to do is spend time with Jesus, and he takes care of the rest.

Jesus goes before us and gives us what we need when we need it. Our job is to receive his love, his truth, and to remain in life-union with him.

## Reflection Questions

Using the tea bag analogy, what belief system has your grief journey released? For me, I had more doubt and unbelief about Jesus' love than I ever realized. The hot water also released feelings of rejection and abandonment.

Who do you need to forgive? Don't forget also to forgive yourself and forgive God if you are holding anger toward him in any way.

What are some practical ways you can start living in daily union with Jesus? (Ideas: Reading your Bible, journaling with Jesus, speaking daily declarations, imagining Jesus with you during your day, worshipping Jesus throughout the day)

## Declarations

- I accept that the pruning in my life is yielding a greater harvest.
- I receive the truth God speaks over me that cleanses me.
- I choose to live my life intimately (into me you see) connected to Jesus.
- I will remain in life-union with Jesus for all of my days, no matter what I face.

## Activation

Imagine yourself with Jesus in a vegetable garden. You are both kneeling down, picking tomatoes from the vine, and placing them in a wooden basket. Feel the warmth of the sun on your skin and Jesus' gentle approach. Look at him and ask him what thoughts and feelings in your soul need his pruning so that you can yield a greater harvest. Write down what he says.

**My Heart Today**

**Prayer**

*Dear Jesus,*

*Thank you for the opportunity to receive your love in a new way today. I choose to live in life-union with you. I give you permission to go deeper and show me how to intimately (into me you see) join my life to yours. What heart pain do I need to release? I forgive you, Jesus, for where I have blamed you. Please forgive me.*

*I want to hear your voice and feel your comfort. Release your peace and your truth in my life. I give you permission to prune my fruitful branches and yield in me a greater harvest. You are my portion, and I can trust you with whatever happens. I love you.*

*In Jesus' name, I pray,*
*Amen*

# Day 26

## Living Powerfully with Jesus

*"I am the sprouting vine and you're my branches. As you live in union with me as your source, fruitfulness will stream from within you—but when you live separated from me you are powerless. If a person is separated from me, he is discarded; such branches are gathered up and thrown into the fire to be burned. But if you live in life-union with me and if my words live powerfully within you—then you can ask whatever you desire and it will be done."*
*John 15:5-7*

No matter what we face in this life, we are still deeply loved by Jesus. Not a distant love but a tangible love, emitting feelings of peace and comfort. Grief comes in waves, but so does this God-given love. One of the first things I said to myself after I called 9-1-1 was, "Well, I guess I'm in the wrong ministry." Nothing could be further from the truth, but I was hit hard with this lie.

For the past few years, I have been blogging about emotional healing. I also led a group of women in Bible study for over five years, where we focused on Bible-based soul healing. I felt like I missed it when Brett took his own life because I didn't help him. Here I was ministering healing for our emotions, and my own husband committed suicide. I had been ministering to him for years. I felt like the rug was pulled out from under me, and my world had flipped upside down.

My new reality of widowhood was challenging everything I once believed. Was God as good as I thought he was before Brett died? How am I going to deal with not seeing my husband, my best friend, every day? How will I support myself now that the breadwinner of our family is gone? There are so many life-altering consequences to losing a spouse. Through it all, Jesus took care of our affairs in ways that just blew me away.

Verse 7 encourages me and reminds me that when we live in life-union with Jesus, and if his words live powerfully within us, then we can ask whatever we desire and it will be done. I can vouch for this, as our every need has been met and then some. We are well taken care of, even though everything has changed.

I do believe God is as good as he was before my husband died. I have also concluded that I am in the right ministry. My faith has been tested and restored. Everything may look different, but Jesus is still the same, and he is pouring out his love on my life like never before.

### Reflection Questions
What questions do you have for Jesus in this season of your life?

What are you grateful for despite the pain of your grief journey?

How has God's love touched your life during this grief journey?

### Declarations
- I am living in life-union with Jesus, and his fruitfulness is within me.
- Jesus' words live powerfully within me.
- I choose to be grateful for my life despite the pain I have suffered.
- I am grateful for (name three things).

## Activation

Each day, you have a choice as to how you will perceive your life. I encourage you to focus on the good that is emerging from your grief season. Since the beginning of this journey, name three good things that have happened in your life. Take a deep breath, recall these moments that brought you joy, and let yourself feel the positive emotions that come with them. Now, write down three things you are grateful for and explain in detail why you are thankful for each one. Let yourself feel the positive emotions. Imagine Jesus with you, enjoying the moment.

## My Heart Today

## Prayer

*Dear Jesus,*

*I choose to receive your love and truth for my life, Jesus. The grief I am experiencing is complicated, and it's challenging my belief system, but I choose to believe you are still good. I have decided to remain in life-union with you despite my tragedy, which has produced my grief. Please continue to speak to me through Scripture and our conversations, and let your words live powerfully in me. Remind me of your love and strengthen me as I draw near to you. Change my perspective and help me to remain grateful. Please help me, Jesus, to remember you when my grief challenges me. I love you and I choose you.*

*In Jesus' name, I pray,*
*Amen*

# Day 27

## Nourishing My Heart with God's Love

*"When your lives bear abundant fruit, you demonstrate that you are
my mature disciples who glorify my Father! "I love each of you with
the same love that the Father loves me. You must continually let my
love nourish your hearts."*
*John 15:8-9*

How do I let Jesus' love nourish my heart? I believe it begins by explor-
ing all of the places where we feel he has abandoned us or let us down.
These places of doubt and unbelief block our hearts from being nourished by Jesus. The secret to happiness is to keep seeking God in each
place where we doubt he is. Our lives cannot bear abundant fruit if we
believe lies about our creator.

There is not one place where God has removed his love for us. Even
facing the death of a loved one, or whatever form of grief you are experiencing as you read this, Jesus is still loving you and caring for you.
He does not abandon us in our pain. Psalm 34:18 says that the Lord is
near to those whose hearts are crushed by pain, and he restores the one
who repents.

When we believe a lie about Jesus, the one who loves us most, we open
the door to deception. The problem with deception is that we don't know
we're being deceived. It is in this place where our lies seem like truth.
When I discovered my husband's body that day in his car, I felt devastated, abandoned, and betrayed. How could my husband do this to
me? But the greater question nagging at my heart was how God could
allow it. I couldn't grasp the fact that my husband wouldn't see our

children again or that I wouldn't hug him again. I was reeling from the enormity of my pain. The shock stayed with me for months. How does someone come back from a blow like this? The answer is one step at a time.

I had to start feeling my feelings and stop avoiding my emotional pain. Jesus showed me that my grief is a gateway to my healing because it was opening up the places in my heart that he wanted to heal. He invited me to trust in him and step into my future with him by my side. Jesus showed me that if I can take these steps, he will heal my heart and use my grief to bear abundant fruit in my life. Grief doesn't have to stay as this awful experience. It can transition us as a fruitful gateway to the next season of our lives.

This is not the way I would have planned it, but as I opened my heart to this new perspective, I began to feel better. Hope was rising in my heart each time I journaled with Jesus about my thoughts. My conversations with him became my lifeline. As a deeper intimacy opened up between me and Jesus, a calming feeling started settling over me. My emotions seemed less heightened, and God's peace was filling my heart. It started with me sharing my deepest thoughts of self-hatred and anger with Jesus. As I released these toxic emotions, the truths began to emerge. I started to feel Jesus' extravagant love even in my grief. Instead of believing these lies of defeat and destruction, my heart opened up to the possibility that Jesus could heal me and my family.

The truth is that Jesus will heal you and your family, too. God doesn't bring us this far to drop us. He's a loving God who uses each trial to cover us in his love if we let him. Look at the promise in James 1:12 about your trial.

*"If your faith remains strong, even while surrounded by life's difficulties, you will continue to experience the untold blessings of God! True happiness comes as you pass the test with faith, and receive the victorious crown of life promised to every lover of God!"*
*James 1:12*

The way to keep your faith strong is to keep the conversation going with Jesus. Speak to him and listen for his response. Read the Word of God, especially the Psalms, and receive his truth.

## Reflection Questions

Where do you feel abandoned or let down by Father God, Jesus, and the Holy Spirit?


Do you feel that your tragedy defines your life? Why or why not?


What belief is hindering God's love from nourishing your heart today?


## Declarations
- I let Jesus' love continually nourish my heart.
- My faith remains strong, even when faced with life's difficulties.
- I live in true happiness, and I receive the victorious crown of life because I am a lover of God.

## Activation

Imagine yourself with Jesus standing at a gate. There is a golden sign on the gate, and it says, "Gateway of Grief." Jesus asks you if you will walk through the gate with him. Picture yourself walking onto this new path, passing through the gate, with Jesus by your side. What do you see? What is Jesus speaking to you? Write down your experience.

## My Heart Today

## Prayer

*Dear Jesus,*

*I ask you to cover me in your love like never before. I give you permission to use my grief as a gateway to my healing. Show me the parts of my heart that are believing a lie. Catapult me out of deception and into your loving arms. I choose to trust you. Uncover the lies I believe and set me free. I want to be a mature disciple who glorifies Father God with my life. I invite you to move supernaturally in my life and set me free. Place me on your path for my life and heal my pain.*

*In Jesus' name, I pray,*
*Amen*

# Day 28

## Sharing In Jesus' Glory

*"For now [Jesus] towers above all creation, for all things exist through him and for him. And that God made him, pioneer of our salvation, perfect through his sufferings, for this is how he brings many sons and daughters to share in his glory."*
*Hebrews 2:10*

If we are to be like Christ, then it is imminent that we will suffer with Christ. The beauty of that suffering is that it brings us into the glory of God. The suffering is actually perfecting us because it is bringing to the surface our true belief system.

The footnote in verse 10 for the word "pioneer" says, "Or "trailblazer" or "forerunner." His perfection through sufferings implies that all his sons will come to glorious perfection through hardships. The Aramaic can be translated "the Prince of Life."[7]

This scripture ministers to me because Jesus was made perfect through his sufferings. It shows me that God can use my pain, the grief of losing my spouse, and all of my unanswered questions to perfect my life. We step into his glory when we trust him to heal our emotional pain. I had no idea how God was going to heal me from such an enormous loss, but he has. It has been this day-by-day, intentional walk with him where I continually stay in conversation with him about the pain arising from my heart. I ask him to show me where this pain started. Then, I go back with him in the memory and ask Jesus to show me his perspective on what happened.

The footnote at the end of verse 10 about the concept of suffering bringing us into the glory of God says, "Or "bring many children into his glorious state." Grace gives us the glory that Jesus has. Although it is true that God will not share his glory with another (Isa. 42:8), but in Christ, we are not "another," we are one with him. See also John 17:22; Rom. 8:29–30."[8]

As a devoted lover of God, we are in Christ. Our salvation puts our name in the Lamb's book of life; we are overcomers, and we experience victory (see Revelation 3:5). Jesus lives in us, helping us every step of the way. He is giving us the grace to face the unimaginable.

Learning that my sufferings can be used for God's glory sparks life in my heart. The very thing that I thought I could not overcome, losing my spouse to suicide, has become my stepping stone. The lies of the enemy are under my feet. I feel stronger than ever, even though I have faced the most significant loss of my life. Only Jesus can do that.

As a follower of Christ, you are a trailblazer and a forerunner for your future generations. Hebrews 2:10 teaches us that we come to glorious perfection through hardships.

## Reflection Questions
How is Jesus perfecting you through your sufferings?


Will you allow Jesus to use your sufferings to bring his glory to your life?


Do you see yourself as an overcomer? Why or why not?


## Declarations
- I am an overcomer and I am victorious.
- I am a trailblazer and a forerunner for my future generations.
- My decision to confront my emotional pain and trust Jesus to transform my life for the better brings glory to God.

- I am perfected through my sufferings.
- I share in Jesus' glory because I follow him and trust him.

## Activation

Write down a list of the situations where you want to achieve victory. For example, I wrote down, "I no longer want to feel rejected, betrayed, or abandoned." Now, ask Jesus to show you his perspective. To me, he said, "Rayna, I was also rejected, betrayed, and abandoned. But my Father God never abandoned me, and he will not abandon you. You are made in my image, and you are deeply loved. Let me show you how much you are loved. You can trust me with your life. I will come through for you every time."

## My Heart Today

## Prayer

*Dear Jesus,*

*Thank you for rescuing me yet again with your truth. You tower above all creation. All things exist through you and for you. Thank you for being the pioneer of my salvation. I ask you to perfect me through my sufferings and allow me to share in your glory.*

*Use my hardships to bring me into glorious perfection in you, Jesus. I know I can't be perfect, but I can have a perfect heart in you. I ask you to use my sufferings to heal and perfect my heart. Show me the way out of my grief and set my feet on solid ground. I love you and I cherish you.*

*In Jesus' name, I pray,*
*Amen*

# Day 29

🔔

## *Fear Will Never Conquer Me*

*"Even when your path takes me through the valley of deepest dark-
ness, fear will never conquer me, for you already have! Your authority
is my strength and my peace. The comfort of your love takes away my
fear. I'll never be lonely, for you are near."*
*Psalm 23:4*

My husband's right arm was tattooed with the words of Psalm 23:4.
Isn't it ironic that the love of my life took his own life with these incredible words staring back at him on his right arm? It's baffling to me that
Brett couldn't feel the great love Jesus had for him and the love from us
as his family and friends. It comforts me that my husband is now surrounded by that same love at this very moment in heaven.

Maybe these words on his arm were meant for me and you? The ones
who would reflect on his life and try to see its meaning. I don't have all
the answers, but I do know this. God's Word holds true no matter what
we face.

I choose to believe God's truth that even in this valley of deep darkness,
fear will not win. As I face my pain, I have decided to choose Jesus as
my conqueror. Because Jesus has conquered my heart, fear cannot. No
matter how much it hurts and feels like fear is conquering my life, I
know the truth that Jesus already conquered fear for me when he went
to the cross.

To overcome the onslaught of fear I was facing, I wrote down each fear and offered it to the Lord. As I wrote, the fears lost their grip on my life. Seeing these lies on a piece of paper loosened their authority in my soul.

My experiences with my Father God, Jesus, and the Holy Spirit were vital in overcoming fear. When I pictured Jesus with me during a particular fear, it started to dissolve. He would speak truth to me and my perspective would change. As the fear reappeared in other parts of my life, I would recall these encounters. These memories with Jesus replaced my old fears with his perfect love.

For example, I always believed I couldn't raise my children without my spouse. When my husband died, I had to confront that fear every day. I realized that it was a lie, and the truth was that I could raise my children on my own. Fear did not defeat me because Jesus was right by my side. Because of my fear, I was creating an imagination that did not include Jesus. Once I surrendered this fear to him, he spoke truth to my heart and comforted me. The truth is that I can overcome all things through Christ (Philippians 4:13). Now I can feel Jesus' presence with me day and night.

I am not lonely because Jesus is near. I want to encourage you to write down your fears and let Jesus speak truth to your heart. You were never meant to live in fear.

### Reflection Questions
What fears are you facing that feel like they will never go away?


What are the counteracting truths to each of these fears?



### Declarations
- God's authority in my life is my strength and my peace.
- Fear will never conquer me because God already has.
- The comfort of God's love takes away my fear.
- I am not alone because Jesus is near me.

## Activation

Write down a list of each fear that is tormenting your life. These are the situations and thoughts/beliefs that cause you anxiety, unrest, and discomfort. Speak the counteracting truth to each fear. For example, one of my fears was that I would not have enough money to support my family. The counteracting truth to this fear is that Jesus takes care of all my needs.

Then I write the scripture: "I am convinced God will fully satisfy my every need, for I have seen the abundant riches of glory revealed to me through Jesus!" Philippians 4:19. Continue this exercise with each fear you are facing. Writing down the fear with its counteracting truth and a scripture anchors it to truth and uproots the lies. The fears lose their grip once they are written down on paper. Once the fears are written down, imagine Jesus sitting next to you and tell him each of your fears. Write down what you perceive he's saying to counteract the fear statements.

## My Heart Today

## Prayer

*Dear Jesus,*

*Thank you that even when your path takes me through the valley of deepest darkness, fear will never conquer me, for you already have conquered fear! I surrender each fear, and I ask you to show me your will for every aspect of my life. I decree that your authority is my strength and my peace. Your sacrifice on the cross was for my healing today.*

*The comfort of your love takes away my fear. I'll never stay lonely, because you are near. I receive your love in this new way today.*

*In Jesus' name, I pray,*
*Amen*

# Day 30

𐬠

## *Possessing Wisdom*

*"God-lovers make the best counselors. Their words possess wisdom
and are right and trustworthy. The ways of God are in their hearts and
they won't swerve from the paths of steadfast righteousness."*
*Psalm 37:30-31*

In my grieving, I have learned that Father God is not some harsh God
trying to make me follow the rules and obey. He's a loving Father who
has my best interest at heart. He wants to hang out with me and see me
succeed and thrive in my life.

One day, after losing my husband, I woke up feeling overwhelmed
about not meeting all the self-imposed demands I had placed on my life.
Demands like: I need to get a job and get over this grief; I need to get
ahead on my laundry; My taxes are not done, and they are due in two
weeks. Then, I gently heard the Holy Spirit speak to me, "Rayna, if you
do nothing more, you're loved just the same. Start to rest in me. Enjoy
your toddler and watch some television. Stop obsessing over getting the
taxes done or finishing the laundry. It will all get done in time. Rest in
me and let me rest in you."

Whoa! It was so refreshing to realize I didn't have to rush around and
meet all these demands from God. His only requests were for me to
believe in him and sit with him. He wanted to get to know me. That's
why this scripture gripped my spirit and opened my eyes to see God
differently.

A true God-lover is a person who knows he or she is loved beyond measure. When you experience that kind of love, you want to release it to others. But it's not a careless, self-serving love. It is the love of a Father whose leading desire is for you to thrive. He's taking each painful moment you encounter and making it good with his healing presence and his wisdom.

I am now walking in the revelation that my heart is safe with Father God. He didn't betray me because my husband committed suicide. He was right by my side, feeling just as sad as I was. I now realize Father God was holding my hand through it all, whispering words of strength and love in my ear. He was ushering me along, assuring me that my kids would still thrive and that my life was being put back together.

As you receive the love of God, it makes you trustworthy and honorable. Steadfast righteousness is not an "I'm right and you're wrong" scenario but a place of deep surrender to Father God because you know you are extremely loved and appreciated. It creates a flow from which you can release God's healing to others as you pray for them and love on them with healthy boundaries.

Your grief journey has placed you in the unique position to minister to others about how Father God has healed your heart.

### Reflection Questions

What wisdom have you gained from God throughout this grief journey?


Will you let God use you to counsel others with his love?


What is the most valuable thing you have learned so far about emotional healing? How will you apply it to your life?

## Declarations

- I am trustworthy and my words possess wisdom.
- The ways of God are in my heart.
- I am using the wisdom I have gained from my grief journey to help others.

## Activation

Write down what you have learned from each piece of wisdom you have gained in your grief journey. For example, I have learned that emotional pain is not equivalent to failure. It means I am human. I also learned that my grief is not a one-way ticket to being doomed forever. Grief is a gateway to healing my deepest heart pains and an opportunity to resolve the pain in my heart and receive healing. After doing that, thank God for healing your heart and ask him to use your pain to help others.

## My Heart Today

## Prayer

*Father God,*

*Your Word says that God-lovers make the best counselors. I want my grief to be used to help others. I ask you to heal my heart and give me the right words to encourage others. Make me trustworthy and release your wisdom to me.*

*I ask you to put your ways in my heart so that I will not swerve from the paths of your steadfast righteousness. Whisper in my ear your words of love and encouragement. Calm my woes and silence my fears so that I am brave enough to share my God experiences.*

*In Jesus' name, I pray,*
*Amen*

# Day 31

⚜

## Tender Love Pursues Me

*"So why would I fear the future? Only goodness and tender love pursue me all the days of my life. Then afterward, when my life is through, I'll return to your glorious presence to be forever with you!"*
*Psalm 23:6*

Several weeks after my husband died, I did this type of trauma therapy where you go back to the scene of your pain and ask Jesus where he was in that moment. I knew I wanted to go to the scene where I was standing next to my husband's car, staring at his lifeless body. I didn't bring my key to his car with me that day, so I couldn't get into his car when I found him. I could only see him through the window. In hindsight, I can see God's protection over my life in allowing me to forget the key. The shock would have been so much worse if I had been able to touch and hold him.

I asked Jesus, "Where were you?" Immediately, I went into a vision, and I saw him standing behind me with his hands on my shoulders. He said, "Rayna, I never wanted this to happen. I will rescue you and your children. I have Brett with me in heaven, and you are not alone." Then I saw him whisk me away to a tree.

As we were sitting under the tree, I was sobbing, and Jesus was comforting me. He was sitting behind me with his hand on my shoulder. In that moment, I felt Jesus' deep sadness. He was as sad as I was for all that was lost because of my husband's suicide. I also received a knowing, deep in my spirit, that Jesus would restore to me everything that was stolen.

As I stayed in the vision, I remembered myself standing next to my husband's car. In that moment, I kept thinking that the love of my life was gone forever, and it felt so hopeless. I didn't know what my world would look like without him, my best friend. Then I realized that the absolute love of my life, Jesus, was standing right next to me the whole time. Because of Jesus' sacrifice on the cross, I would see my husband again in heaven. Until then, I have a race to run and a divine destiny to fulfill. So do you.

My story is not over, and my happy ending is still out there. I know that Brett would want me to receive heart healing and to enjoy my life. Jesus has never left your side either. He's right there with you, placing his hands on your shoulders and interceding his blessings and his hope into your life. I encourage you to ask him where he was when your grief began.

### Reflection Questions
What memory keeps popping into your head when you think about your grief journey?

Will you invite Jesus into the memory?

Where was Jesus when your grief began?

### Declarations
- I do not fear the future because Jesus is with me.
- The tender love of Jesus is with me always.
- Goodness pursues me all the days of my life.

### Activation
Allow yourself to remember the scene associated with the start of your grief—the time and place you first learned about it. Take a deep breath and look around to see where Jesus is standing in that scene. Notice what he's doing, where he's standing, and what he might be saying to you. If you're having trouble visualizing him, remember that it's as simple as imagining yourself walking to your car, opening the door, and

sitting in the driver's seat. You can reread Appendix B for a reminder on how to imagine yourself with Jesus. Wait for him and ask him to speak to you. Write down what you experience. What does Jesus have to say about your memory?

## My Heart Today

## Prayer

*Dear Jesus,*

*I repent for fearing the future. Thank you for revealing to me your truth that your goodness and tender love pursue me all the days of my life. Please give me the strength and determination to fulfill my God-given destiny and purpose. When my race is done, I'll return to your glorious presence in heaven to be forever with you.*

*Until then, I ask you to lead me and guide me in your ways. Strengthen me with your perspective and heal my heart. Redirect my thoughts and emotions to bring me into truth. Give me your peace and clarity about my future.*

*In Jesus' name, I pray,*
*Amen*

# Day 32

🔥

## *Living In God's Presence*

*"Don't be obsessed with money but live content with what you have, for you always have God's presence. For hasn't he promised you, 'I will never leave you, never! And I will not loosen my grip on your life!' So we can say with great confidence: 'I know the Lord is for me and I will never be afraid of what people may do to me!'"*
*Hebrews 13:5-6*

Another battle in my season of grief is navigating how to respond when I feel two opposing feelings simultaneously. How can I be so mad at my spouse and love him so much at the same time? For example, I will feel relief that my spouse is in heaven and no longer in pain while also feeling a deep yearning to have him back and hold his hand again.

I hate how final death is. It hurts deeply to realize I can't hug my precious husband again. I get so sad that I can't give him a face-to-face, heartfelt apology for every time I hurt his feelings. I just want to look into his eyes and say I love you one more time. Suicide has robbed me of these things.

The truth is that we don't know how many years, days, hours, or minutes we have with any of our loved ones. Because of losing my spouse so suddenly, I am learning to cherish the moment and acknowledge Jesus' presence in every situation. I love the promise from verse 5, "I will never leave you, never! And I will not loosen my grip on your life!" As I reflect on these words, the grip of abandonment, rejection, and betrayal melts away.

Another important part of this verse is accepting the truth that I never need to fear what people might do to me. My husband left me in such a dramatic, horrific way that it instilled fear in my heart. At first, I expressed this fear through anger, but once I got to the root of it, I realized I was dealing with the fear of being abandoned. My husband certainly abandoned me, but I find comfort in knowing that the Lord is for me. I don't have to depend on my husband or anyone else to meet my needs. Jesus will meet all my needs because he will never abandon me. Embracing this truth and letting it take root in my heart gave me the strength to forgive my husband for what he did.

In my grieving process, I have discovered a new truth about Jesus. My skepticism and doubt have been replaced with this deep knowing that the Lord is for me. I have an understanding in my heart that I don't have to be afraid of what anyone in my life does, including my spouse committing suicide, because I am not alone. Jesus is by my side, and he's making everything right again. I encourage you to ask Jesus to replace fear and doubt with a knowing that he will never loosen his grip of love on your life.

## Reflection Questions
Do you sometimes feel two conflicting feelings at the same time? What are they?

Do you feel skeptical about whether or not Jesus will come through for you? Why or why not?

Are you afraid someone else is going to do something you can't handle? Explain and ask God for his opinion.

## Declarations
- God will never leave me, ever!
- God is for me and not against me.
- God will never loosen his grip on my life.
- I say with great confidence, God is for me.

## Activation

List every area of your life where you feel skeptical about whether Jesus will come through for you. For example, paying off your credit card bills, covering school tuition, or restoring your relationships. Imagine you and Jesus sitting across from one another at a conference table. Ask Jesus for his opinion about each situation and write down his response.

## My Heart Today

## Prayer

*Dear Jesus,*

*Thank you for always being with me. Even if I don't tangibly feel you all the time, I know you are here with me because of what you said in Hebrews 13:5-6. I want to draw closer to you in my grief process. Thank you, Jesus, for never leaving me! I am so grateful that you do not loosen your grip on my life, no matter what I face! I decree that Jesus is for me, and I will never be afraid of what people may do to me.*

*I repent about feeling skeptical about you, and I ask you to forgive me. I choose to place my faith, my trust, and my confidence in Jesus from this day forward. Open my heart to learn new truths about your intentions for my life. Thank you for protecting me every step of the way in my grief journey.*

*In Jesus' name, I pray,*
*Amen*

# Day 33

🔱

## *Walking Down Rescue Road*

*"Out of my deep anguish and pain I prayed, and God, you helped
me as a father. You came to my rescue and broke open the way into a
beautiful and broad place. Now I know, Lord, that you are for me, and
I will never fear what man can do to me."*
*Psalm 118:5-6*

During my intense struggle with blaming myself for my husband's suicide, I talked to my grief counselor, and she opened my eyes to a different perspective. She said, "It's scarier to recognize that we are not in
control over bad things happening in our lives than it is to blame ourselves. That's where the 'it's my fault' thoughts come in." Wow! This
hit home in so many ways.

It is so much easier to blame myself than to live in a world where I am
not in control, and tragedy could happen at any moment. This makes
perfect sense to me. My heart could not handle accepting the finality of
my husband's suicide, so I put myself through the severe self-sabotage
of blaming myself.

There are many conversations with my husband where I wish I had
responded differently or had a better attitude toward him. But the truth
is, it was never my responsibility to keep my husband alive. This false
responsibility had ruled my life long enough. I was done with the feelings of guilt and shame, and I was ready to find a resolution in my heart.

I am also reminded of God's role in all of this. Who am I to say that it
was my place to keep God's son alive? If God allowed him to die and go

to heaven, I need to accept that. Of course, it's so much easier said than done, but at the end of the day, it all comes down to trust.

Do I trust Father God? Do I believe that he has my best interest at heart? Am I living in the truth that I am safe, loved, and cared for by my Father God? These scriptures in Psalm 118:5-6 minister to my heart because they emphasize how God helps me as a father.

God is rescuing me and breaking open the way to the next season of my life. But I have to receive it. He's doing the same for you. Will you accept his invitation? I believe that when you do, you will begin to lose the fear of man because that fear is replaced with the truth that God is for us.

### Reflection Questions
What are you still blaming yourself for in your grief journey?

In what ways are you engaging in self-sabotage in your life?

Do you trust Father God with your grief journey? Why or why not?

How is God helping you as a Father in your grief journey?

### Declarations
* God helps me as a father. I am safe, cared for, and loved.
* God rescues me and breaks open new paths for my life.
* God is for me; I will never fear what man can do to me.

### Activation
Imagine yourself with Father God at a construction site. You are helping him pour concrete onto a new road he is building. You ask Father God, "Where will this road lead?" He answers, "This is your rescue road. I am pouring out a new path for you to take. It's a path of healing where your grief turns into a gift of vulnerability."

Now ask Father God to tell you about your rescue road. Write down what you receive.

## My Heart Today

## Prayer

*Father God,*

*I repent for self-sabotage and for blaming myself for the circumstances of my grief. Please forgive me for taking matters into my own hands and for blaming myself instead of trusting you with my broken heart. Please heal my heart and continue your deep work within me.*

*Transform me into the person you created me to be. It's never too late with you, Jesus. Thank you for understanding that in my deep anguish and pain, I can pray and you will help me. I ask you to come to my rescue and break open my life to a new, beautiful place. Teach me deep in my heart that you are for me. As this truth resonates in my heart, fill me up with your promise that I will never fear what man can do to me.*

*In Jesus' name, I pray,*
*Amen*

# Day 34

✦

## *Triumphing Over My Enemies*

*"For you stand beside me as my hero who rescues me. I've seen with my own eyes the defeat of my enemies. I've triumphed over them all! Lord, it is so much better to trust in you to save me than to put my confidence in someone else."*
*Psalm 118:7-8*

Seven-and-a-half months after my husband died, I spent the night alone at my house for the first time. My toddler is now old enough to sleep over at a family member's home, and I had a head cold, so when my family offered to take her for the night, I said yes. I watched a movie and relaxed, but I couldn't help but notice how eerily quiet it was in my house. I heard every crack and squeak after I turned off the television. My senses were heightened, and needless to say, I couldn't sleep.

Death is so final, and the aftermath solidifies that. Without my consent, I have been thrown into this world of being a single mom and navigating family life without a husband. I feel so vulnerable, and I realize just how codependent I was with my husband. There are so many things that I relied on him for, even in his sickness.

A false refuge is anything we prioritize over God that provides us comfort. It might be overeating candy, streaming shows for hours at a time, excessive shopping, or being codependent on a loved one. The idea is that I turn to this false refuge for comfort instead of going to God.

Reading Psalm 118:7, I am reminded that Father God is my hero who rescues me, not my husband Brett. Even if my husband were here, it's wrong for me to put all my trust in him and bypass God's role in my life. I've never been left alone by God. He always rescues me and gives me victory over my enemies. Those enemies are the fear laced in every noise I hear when the lights go out at night and the silent whispers telling me that I am all alone.

The truth is, we are never alone as children of God, and I choose to put my confidence in him. Will you choose the same?

### Reflection Questions
What or who are you using as a false refuge?

When do you turn to this false refuge for comfort? Is there a trigger?

What enemies are you facing? (i.e., fear, rejection, loneliness, or disappointment)

### Declarations
- I put my confidence in Father God; my trust is in you, God.
- Father God stands beside me as my hero who rescues me.
- I will triumph over all my enemies.

### Activation
Write down your false refuges and ask God to forgive you for putting them before him in your life. Ask Father God to reveal the trigger that causes you to turn to these false refuges. A trigger is a trauma response, and it happens when a current experience "triggers" your brain to remember a past trauma, causing your body to respond the same way it did during the original trauma. Now ask God to fill you with his love in this area of your life and to speak truth to every lie you believed. Choose to place your confidence in Father God and not in your false refuges.

## My Heart Today

## Prayer

*Father God,*

*I repent for each false refuge (list each one) in my life. Please forgive me for putting idols before you. I agree with Psalm 118:7-8, and I receive you, Father God, to stand by my side as my hero who rescues me.*

*I want to see with my own eyes the defeat of my enemies. Help me to triumph over them all! No longer will fear, loneliness, rejection, disappointment, or (add other negative emotions you are dealing with) be left undefeated. For it is so much better to trust in you, Father God, to save me than to put my confidence in someone else. I trust you with every area of my life.*

*In Jesus' name, I pray,*
*Amen*

# Day 35

🛐

## *My Tears Become Liquid Words*

*"Lord, listen to all my tender cries. Read my every tear, like liquid words that plead for your help. I feel all alone at times, like a stranger to you, passing through this life just like all those before me. Don't let me die without restoring joy and gladness to my soul. May your frown over my failure become a smile over my success."*
*Psalm 39:12-13*

Thinking of my tears as liquid words that plead for God's help brings me comfort. I can't count how many nights I've gone to bed crying, or mornings I've woken up to tears since my husband's death. I remember during that time thinking to myself, "When will my tears stop flowing all day and even into the night?"

The answer is different for every person. For me, it took time because the suicide was such a shock. As my grief counselor explained to me, I didn't have a grid in my brain for this loss. It was a sudden loss versus an anticipated loss, which made it all the more difficult. Then, on top of the shock, there was the reality of how he left this earth. I just never imagined that suicide would be part of our story.

I guess I thought I loved him too much for something like this to happen to us. In fact, I have no idea what I thought, except that God was going to heal my husband. God did heal my husband because he's in heaven, free of pain. It's just the path to get there that messes with me.

Reconciling the two facts of Brett being healed and Brett committing suicide jars my heart. This scripture speaks to me because the psalmist asks God not to let him die without restoring his joy and bringing gladness to his soul. I relate to that because I don't want to cry forever.

I want to get to a place where God smiles over my success. I have failed in so many ways, including in my marriage. I wish I could have saved my husband, but the reality is that it was not in my control. As hard as it is, I now accept that. Brett's decision was independent of my decision.

Let's surrender all our tears to Jesus and ask him to heal us.

## Reflection Questions
Have you ever considered your tears to be liquid words that plead for your help? How does this change your perspective on crying?

What situation are you crying to sleep over?

Will you surrender the situation to Father God so he can help? Why or why not?

## Declarations
- God reads my every tear like liquid words pleading for his help.
- God is restoring joy and gladness to my soul.
- God smiles over my success for my success is in him.

## Activation
What is most shocking to you about your grief journey? Sit with Jesus in your favorite place. This could be a park you grew up going to, the beach, or the mountains. Ask him to show you how he will restore joy and gladness to your soul. Sit with the answer until you feel a positive emotion. Write down your experience.

**My Heart Today**

**Prayer**

*Dear Jesus,*

*I ask you to listen to all my tender cries and read my every tear, like liquid words that plead for your help. I feel all alone at times, like a stranger to you, passing through this life. Please show me your presence in my life and heal my spirit, soul, and body. Quiet my heart and give me the answers I'm seeking at every moment.*

*Don't let me die without restoring joy and gladness to my soul. I pray that you will restore my failures and smile over my successes. I choose to focus on my future while still honoring my past. Heal my heart, Jesus. I love you, and I trust you to complete your work in me.*

*In Jesus' name, I pray,*
*Amen*

# Day 36

## Comforting Others in Their Suffering

*"He always comes alongside us to comfort us in every suffering so
that we can come alongside those who are in any painful trial. We can
bring them this same comfort that God has poured out upon us."*
*2 Corinthians 1:4*

My empathy for others has increased significantly since my season of
grieving my husband's loss. I see this as another gift that grief has given
me. While I don't wish a grief season on anyone, the comfort I've received from Father God has been life-changing. Now I want to give that
same comfort to others. It is one of my primary motivations for publishing this devotional. If my pain can help someone else, then it was worth
it. I have been comforted by Father God, so I want others to know they
can be comforted too.

Many times, God sends people into your life to comfort you during your
times of suffering. My dear sister and friends have continuously encouraged me on my grief journey, reminding me of my identity in Christ and
that I have a bright future. They have prayed with me and loved on me
when I couldn't love myself. I want to encourage you to stay connected
with others. If you're alone, get connected with your local church community or a grief group.

My grief has strengthened my trust in Father God, and that has transformed my outlook on many parts of my life. I used to struggle with
intense social anxiety, and I was constantly worried about what others thought of me. This vanity was something I hated, and it caused
me pain.

But now, after experiencing God's pure love during my grief, the social anxiety has decreased significantly. I now know that I can dissect my thought life and get to the bottom of every issue I face. I feel comfortable being vulnerable with Father God and sharing with him my deepest fears and problems.

Reflecting on your negative emotions, uncovering the root of your pain, meeting with Jesus, and bringing your thoughts, beliefs, and feelings into the truth of God's Word is life-changing. Grief gave me the gift of no longer being able to ignore my negative emotions. Of course, at first, I did not think this was a gift. I was angry and just wanted it to stop. But the pain of sudden grief was so loud, I had to face it. In retrospect, that was a gift. I am also humbled knowing that this process of healing will continue for the rest of my life.

As I heal, I have developed a new sense of empathy and compassion for others seeking healing. I now see it as an honor to walk alongside those who are grieving. If my struggles can help you in any way, I am truly grateful. Nothing is wasted with God. He uses everything for his glory. My prayer is that you, too, will be able to help others someday. As you choose to heal your heart now, God will use you in the future to support someone else. Our pain is never wasted when God is at our side.

### Reflection Questions
Look back at the last few months of your life. How have you been comforted by others?


How can you help others now that you have grieved at this deep level?


What do you want someone else to learn about grief?


### Declarations
- Father God always comes alongside me and comforts me.
- I have empathy for others, and I comfort them where I can.
- I trust Father God, no matter what life throws my way.

## Activation

Let's sit with Father God and thank him for rescuing us. Imagine you and him at a coffee shop drinking a hot tea, cappuccino, or your favorite coffee treat. Share with him two or three instances where he has rescued you and shown you kindness and comfort during your grief journey, and express your heartfelt gratitude. Then, write how being rescued inspires you to help others. Thank him in your own way for his role in rescuing you. Ask Father God what he has to say about your future. Write down his response.

## My Heart Today

## Prayer

*Father God,*

*Thank you for always coming alongside me to comfort me in every suffering. You are so loving, and you meet all of my needs. Teach me how to receive your comfort so that my heart can heal.*

*As I heal, I want to share my journey with others. I want to walk alongside those who are in painful trials and let them know they will receive the same comfort you have poured out upon me. Give me a heart of empathy for others, Lord. Heal my heart and make me a person who can help someone else become an overcomer.*

*In Jesus' name, I pray,*
*Amen*

# Day 37

🔻

## *God Is My Stronghold*

*"But as for me, your strength shall be my song of joy. At each and every sunrise, my lyrics of your love will fill the air! For you have been my glory-fortress, a stronghold in my day of distress."*
*Psalm 59:16*

I have a friend who lost her husband to suicide about five years before me. She has been a great resource in my grief journey. One day, when I was with her and she boldly said, "I'm glad my husband committed suicide. If that's what he wanted, then who am I to say no to it?" This was about five months after I lost my husband. I was baffled by her comment, but I tried to be understanding as I knew she was further along in processing her grief than I was.

About six months after my husband died, I started writing this book. As I wrote, my thoughts became clearer, and I began to understand my own heart. I realized I was blaming myself for many things that were out of my control. I also felt the need to let Brett go in a healthy way. I wanted to respect his choice to leave this earth despite all the pain it caused.

A few weeks later, I was at lunch with some of my girlfriends, and I found myself saying that I understood why my husband took his own life. I also mentioned that I was beginning to feel like I'm okay with it. I further explained that I feel like I might even be thankful someday. As soon as I said the words, I wished I could take them back. Guilt gushed over me like a steamroller. My tears started flowing, and I couldn't stop crying. I just sat with my grief and allowed myself to feel my emotions out in public at that restaurant table.

That night, I only slept for five hours. I stayed awake, thinking about what I said and battling with guilt. I was frustrated because I couldn't sleep a full night for the fifth consecutive day, and I asked God to show me why. Then, I remembered my friend saying she was glad her husband committed suicide. Now I understand.

Suicide has so many unsaid social norms around it. Like, don't say anything bad about the person who died, or don't bring it up in happy social situations. Certainly, don't say you're glad they did it or you're thankful. But I would like to slash these unsaid rules and just be real. Our life was hard. My husband's chronic pain was terrible. The fact that he doesn't have to live in pain gives me relief. I am thankful that he is not in pain anymore. Also, I am personally grateful that I get a new start. There, I said it.

You get a new start, too. Your life is happening for you, not to you. When we truly grasp this idea, we can see God's love in all things. By being honest with ourselves, God's strength becomes our song of joy. As our glory fortress, Jesus becomes our place of protection, strength, and triumph. When we trust Jesus, we give him a stronghold on our lives, and then we can heal. He's healing us with every step of vulnerability and honesty. I encourage you to give yourself permission to get real.

**Reflection Questions**
What are some unsaid social norms surrounding your grief journey?


What is the reality surrounding your grief?


Were you in a challenging situation before the grief?


How can you take steps toward a new start?


**Declarations**
- God's strength shall be my song of joy.
- I declare that my life is happening for me and not to me.

- God is my stronghold in my day of distress.
- I am building a new life, and I am starting to enjoy it.

## Activation

Imagine boarding a plane, putting your bags in the overhead compartment, and then sitting down in your seat, only to realize Jesus is seated next to you. Look over at him and say hello. Now picture Jesus as your stronghold with his hand extended toward you. He's the one who lifts you up and offers guidance in your times of distress. Hold his hand and ask him what he has to say about your unexpected new beginning in life and moving forward despite your grief. Write down his response.

## My Heart Today

## Prayer

*Dear Jesus,*

*Please help me to continue to be honest with myself and vulnerable with my feelings. Don't let me conform to social norms that are keeping me stuck in pent-up pain. Please help me express myself and understand the root of my issues.*

*Give me the strength to feel the things that are not socially acceptable and to face difficult social situations. I choose for your strength to be my song of joy. Break me free from people-pleasing and abandoning myself. I want to feel my feelings. Also, I want to feel your love at every moment.*

*Jesus, you are my glory fortress and my stronghold in my day of distress. I will lean on you and glean from your wisdom, strength, and courage for the rest of my days.*

*Thank you for being with me in my grief and for changing my perspec-*
*tive. My grief has been a gift of vulnerability and getting to know myself*
*in a new way. My grief journey has turned into a Jesus journey, and I*
*never want it to stop. Pour your love into my heart and soul like never*
*before. Let's do this.*

*In Jesus' name, I pray,*
*Amen*

# Day 38

⚜

## *Becoming Spiritually Mature*

*"So don't be impatient for YAHWEH to act; keep moving forward*
*steadily in his ways, and he will exalt you to possess the land. You'll*
*watch with your own eyes and see the wicked lose everything. But you*
*can tell who are the blameless and spiritually mature. What a differ-*
*ent story with them! The godly ones will have a peaceful, prosperous*
*future with a happy ending."*
*Psalm 37:34, 37*

When I think about possessing the land, it reminds me of a civil war. Two parties that both claim ownership of the land must fight for their rights to possess it. In this case, the two parties are godly and ungodly thoughts: truths and lies. Our job is to steadily move forward in God's ways. We do this by learning about who God is and what he thinks of us. Then we learn to discern which thoughts are from him and which are from our flesh or the devil.

The grief journey is up and down. The smallest things, like making meatballs for my children, could set me back. I would be crying in the kitchen because the last time I made these meatballs, my husband was eating them. I have learned to allow myself to grieve. It is so sad that my husband and our family will never eat meatballs together again. How-ever, I have to make the choice not to dwell in the pain. There's a fine line between grief and self-pity. I don't want to find myself in the pit of self-sabotage by dwelling on the negative thought that I was all alone without my husband.

My grief exposed the battle in my mind for God's truth. As I accepted the truth rather than the lies of the enemy, peace filled my heart. I questioned so much of my thinking and discovered that I had many doubts about God's love for me. If he loves me so much, then why is my life so hard? But again, this thinking is a trap. Everyone's life is hard in one way or another.

When verse 34 says, "You'll watch with your own eyes and see the wicked lose everything," I believe it is referring to the battle in your mind. When the wicked lose, everyone wins. Some of the wicked things we battle are self-pity, depression, anxiety, or anger. These things have no life in them, but when we choose to act on them, we harm ourselves and the people we love.

Spending time with the Lord taught me that even though I feel sad about missing my husband, I don't have to agree with wicked things. I have the choice to feel my feelings, process my thoughts, and then release them to Jesus.

My goal is to become spiritually mature. Verse 37 says, "What a different story with them! The godly ones will have a peaceful, prosperous future with a happy ending." What I entertain in my thought life will determine whether I will possess the land. It is a battle in our minds for truth. When our thoughts align with God's truth, his glory is released through us.

Once we know the truth, it can set us free. John 8:32 says, "For if you embrace the truth, it will release true freedom into your lives." The freedom comes when our belief system lines up with God's belief system.

The beauty in all of it is that Father God is this incredible, loving God who genuinely cares for each one of us. Father God wants the best for each one of us, but we have to come into agreement with his ways for us to possess the land.

## Reflection Questions

What lies are you believing that are hindering you from a joyful future? If you can't think of any, ask Jesus to reveal them to you.

What is the truth behind each of these lies?

What areas of your life still feel hopeless?

What does a happy ending look like for you? Explain.

## Declarations

- I am spiritually mature.
- I choose to take responsibility for my emotions and deal with them.
- I release my negative emotions to Jesus.
- I have a peaceful and prosperous future.
- From this day forward, my life will be joyful and I believe I will have a happy ending.

## Activation

Be encouraged that each day you are becoming more spiritually mature. Identify the areas of your life that still feel hopeless and where you doubt God's love for you. Picture yourself sitting just outside a cozy, wooden mountain cabin. The sun has set, and night has fallen. The mountain air is cold and crisp. Close your eyes and imagine sitting next to Jesus in a wooden chair by a fire, surrounded by rocks to contain it. You both have on warm coats, boots, and a blanket. Ask Jesus for his opinion about the hopelessness and doubt you struggle with. Now ask him about your happy ending. What does he have to say?

**My Heart Today**

**Prayer**

*Father God,*

*Teach me how to continually examine my thoughts and bring them into alignment with the truth of your Word. Help me become familiar with your ways in every area of my life. Reveal the hopelessness within me and set me free. Show me where I am entertaining lies from the enemy or my flesh. I invite you to share your thoughts with me so I can learn from your perspective. I want to grow and become spiritually mature. I choose to spend this time with you today to learn more about you. I love you, Father God. Thank you for loving me and teaching me your truths.*

*In Jesus' name, I pray,*
*Amen*

# Day 39

Becoming a River of Flowing Water

*"Then on the most important day of the feast, the last day, Jesus stood and shouted out to the crowds—'All you thirsty ones, come to me! Come to me and drink! Believe in me so that rivers of living water will burst out from within you, flowing from your innermost being, just like the Scripture says!'"*
*John 7:37-38*

Water is a cleansing agent. It can be powerful and destructive, like in a hurricane, or it can be a nourishing source of life that quenches your thirst. Jesus is the living water. He can be anything and everything we need him to be, no matter what we face. We only have to believe, and he will do the rest.

Jesus has cleansed my soul by bringing his truth to the lies I was believing. He has powerfully pierced my heart with his relentless love, compassion, and comfort. My soul has been nourished back to life through my journaling and communion with him. He's never left my side.

The emotional pain and stressful moments after my husband's passing sometimes seemed louder than Jesus' presence, but Jesus was always there. The footnote about the last day of the feast in verse 37 says, "When man's feasting is over there is still thirst. Jesus comes at the last day of the feast to satisfy the thirst of those who seek God. Only the Lord Jesus can quench the spiritual thirst of men by giving them his living water."[9]

The living water of Jesus is what I was craving in my grief as I faced the days ahead. I didn't know it at the time, but I've learned in this process that I was created for his living water, and I was naturally gravitating towards it in my grief. Only Jesus could quench this thirst in my heart. I was having an epiphany of his love as I grieved in my darkest valley. I met with Jesus, voicing my deepest emotions and irrational thoughts. His response was to give me answers and provide comfort for my soul. I encourage you to continue to open your heart to Jesus for the rest of your life. Get real with him and hear what he has to say.

Verse 38 says that as we believe in Jesus, rivers of living water will burst out from within us. The footnote at the end of verse 38 says, "Or 'rivers of living water will flow from his throne within.' See Isa. 44:3; 55:1; 58:11; Ezek. 47:1; Rev. 22:1. A drink becomes a river!"[10]

Because of salvation, Jesus lives inside us, and because of that, his throne is within us. If we allow it, his living waters can become a river, not just a drink, flowing from his throne to the deepest parts of our souls where we need him most. This is a lifelong journey we undertake with Jesus as the lead. He's guiding us to victory; our role is to receive.

Put your hand in front of your face and breathe on it. Jesus is as close to you as your breath. His living waters are just waiting for an invitation into your heart.

### Reflection Questions
Do you want Jesus' river of living water to flow through you?


Ask Jesus to show you any places in your heart that are dry and ask him to quench them.


Ask Jesus to fill you with his relentless love, compassion, and comfort. Write down his response.

## Declarations

- Jesus has cleansed my soul.
- I am a river of flowing water.
- I am filled with Jesus' relentless love, compassion, and comfort.
- My soul has been nourished back to life by Jesus.

## Activation

Imagine standing in front of a waterfall, with rushing water splashing onto your hands and bouncing everywhere, soaking everything around you. Your feet, hands, and clothes are all wet. Water drips from your hair, and you feel the refreshment. Look to your right and see Jesus enjoying the waterfall with you. Ask him for more of his living water. Write down what you experience.

## My Heart Today

## Prayer

*Dear Jesus,*

*I invite your river of living water to pour into my soul and soothe the emotional pain I'm experiencing. Help me to be vulnerable and open my heart to you. I believe this is the missing part of my healing journey. I ask you to fill my heart and soul with your river of living water and your comforting love. I know you are as close as my breath, and I want to feel you in this way. I open my heart to you in this new way. Meet with me, Jesus, and teach me your ways.*

*In Jesus' name, I pray,*
*Amen*

# Day 40

🌿

## *Restored By God*

*"And then, after your brief suffering, the God of all loving grace, who has called you to share in his eternal glory in Christ, will personally and powerfully restore you and make you stronger than ever. Yes, he will set you firmly in place and build you up."*
*1 Peter 5:10*

In 2008, when my husband was in his 30s, he was in a car accident that changed his life forever. Never again would he have a day without physical pain. When I think about this, it creates a deep empathy in my heart for what he was going through. Then, after 2020, he got long COVID, had a stroke, and began to deal with debilitating anxiety and depression. Oh, how he suffered!

Now, as his wife facing a life without him, I am suffering. But Jesus' promise holds true. First Peter 5:10 clearly states that Father God, the God of all loving grace, will personally and powerfully restore me and make me stronger than ever. It says that he will set me firmly in place and build me up. He will do the same for you.

As we close these 40 days of dealing with our grief and searching our hearts for truth, I hope you are encouraged and transformed by the truth of God's word. I am always surprised at how many scriptures refer to suffering and brokenness. But my joy lies in the promises of victory and triumph that are always the conclusion to emotional pain. I am so thankful that Jesus changed my perspective and showed me that my grief is a gift and a catalyst for my healing and growth.

In the Bible, the number 40 symbolizes trials, testing, and healing. It's the kind of healing that prepares you for the next chapter of life. This is seen in several biblical accounts, including the story of Jesus spending 40 days fasting before starting his public ministry (see Matthew 4:1-11).

My prayer is that these 40 days have purified your heart with the truth of God's Word. I pray you would take Jesus at his word and let him in to heal your heart so you can enter the next season that God has for you.

My question from the beginning arises again. Will you let your grief anchor you to darkness or catapult you into growth? I'm choosing growth, and you have too! Thank you for joining me on this journey of personal growth and freedom. It is my honor and a great privilege to speak into your life. May Jesus bless you abundantly as you continue to abide in him.

## Reflection Questions

What victories are you experiencing now?

What areas of your life will you now live in triumph over since starting this devotional?

How has your grief been a catalyst for your healing and personal growth?

## Declarations

- My heart is purified by the truth of God's Word.
- Jesus is healing my heart today and forever.
- I will use my healing to offer compassion and empathy to others.
- I am restored by Jesus and stronger than ever.
- God has set me firmly in place and he is building me up.

## Activation

Write down three victories you are experiencing now that you have taken this journey with Jesus to let your grief become a gift. For example, some of my victories are (1) I no longer cry myself to sleep at night, (2) I feel hope each morning, and I do not fear my future, and (3) I feel comfortable in social situations, and the social anxiety is 90% better. Now sit with Jesus and thank him for how far you have come with him by your side. Ask him to speak to you about your future. Write down what you experience.

## My Heart Today

## Prayer

*Dear Jesus,*

*Thank you for changing my perception of grief and its purpose. I give you my permission to continue to use my grief to show me the pain in my heart and the lies I am believing. Give me your perspective on my life.*

*Heal my pain and bring me into my next season. Now I know I can still have a future despite my grief. Thank you for personally and powerfully restoring me and making me stronger than ever. I receive your love that is setting me firmly in place and building me up for my destiny and future. I choose to walk in the truth that with you by my side, I can do anything I need to do. I love you, Jesus, and I never could have made it this far without you.*

*I look forward to my future because of you.*

*In Jesus' name, I pray,*
*Amen*

# A Letter to My Late Husband

Dear Brett,

I don't think I will ever fully understand your departure from this world on this side of heaven. I'm coming to terms with that, and I accept that I can't know everything or figure it all out. I'm sorry I didn't save you. I now realize it wasn't my role to save you, so I guess I should say I'm sorry you weren't saved from suicide. I also understand that you didn't see any hope left for yourself in this world, which makes me so sad.

I know you wouldn't want me to stay this sad, so I am seeking Jesus for his answers on how to overcome the hopelessness of your absence. I accept that we only had nine years and ten months together on this earth. What you did for me during that time will always be a treasure to me. You made me a wife and a mom on the same day. Being a stepmom to our boys is a lifelong dream come true. Then you made me a mother to our daughter, and I was able to experience pregnancy and nursing; all gifts I never would have had without you. **But the greatest gift was you.**

You were my best friend, and I will really miss having you by my side. I am so sorry you endured so much pain in this life. I find comfort in knowing you are no longer suffering. I am also sorry that I was so angry with you after you died. I forgive you for taking your life and leaving us. I bless you to fulfill your destiny in heaven for all of eternity.

Thank you for praying and interceding for us. We are going to make it. I love you with all my heart.

Your wife,
Rayna

Dear Reader,

I encourage you to write a letter either to your deceased loved one or to Jesus about your grief journey as a way to cope and find healing. My prayer is that you will heal from your pain and develop a positive outlook on life.

From my heart to yours,
Rayna

# Appendix A

## List of Negative Emotions & The Opposite Positive Emotions

| | |
|---|---|
| Abandoned | Supported, Loved |
| Aggravated | Calm |
| Angry | Peaceful, Forgiving |
| Annoyed | Satisfied, Delightful |
| Anxiety | Peace |
| Betrayed | Faithful, Loyal |
| Bitter | Content, Joyful |
| Brokenhearted | Wholehearted, Healing Your Heart |
| Denial | Accepting |
| Depressed | Joyful, Hopeful |
| Disappointment | Satisfied, Pleased |
| Disgust | Lovely, Attracted To |
| Fearful | Peaceful, Loved |
| Frustration | Contentment, Fulfillment |
| Grief | Joy |
| Guilt | Innocent |
| Hate | Love |
| Hostility | Friendliness |
| Jealousy | Understanding, Loving, Accepting |
| Lonely | Belonging, Connection |
| Neglected | Cherished, Adored, Valued |
| Overwhelmed | Calm, In Control, At Ease |
| Rejected | Accepted |
| Sad | Happy |
| Shame | Known, Accepted, Compassion |
| Stressed | Peaceful, At Ease |

# Appendix B

## How to Use Your Imagination to See God

God gave us our imagination as a gift to see into the spirit realm. As we get older and become more analytical, we often lose sight of this gift, which resides in the right side of the brain. Your imagination functions like spiritual eyes, allowing you to perceive the spirit realm. When Jesus talks about becoming like a child in Matthew 18:3, he's referencing a "little child," and small children frequently use their imagination.

*"Learn this well: Unless you dramatically change your way of thinking and become teachable like a little child, you will never be able to enter in."*
*Matthew 18:3*

We are called to reframe our thinking and adopt a childlike perspective to enter the kingdom of heaven. Children constantly use their imaginations, which fuel their creativity. Similarly, many inventions and discoveries have originated from someone using their imagination. The imagination is a powerful part of our minds, capable of shaping our destiny—either positively or negatively.

Another key scripture to consider is Isaiah 26:3, which says that peace surrounds those whose imaginations are consumed with God. It creates confident trust just as the scripture says.

*"Perfect, absolute peace surrounds those whose imaginations are consumed with you; they confidently trust in you."*
*Isaiah 26:3*

The footnote in The Passion Translation by Dr. Brian Simmons for the word "imaginations" in Isaiah 26:3 is: "Or 'steadfast minds.' The Hebrew is yêtser. According to the Brown-Driver-Briggs Hebrew Lexicon, the Hebrew word yêtser means 'imagination' that forms and frames up. Imagination frames up one's reality. It is unfortunate that many today have rejected the God-created imagination that each of us possesses. Our imagination must be set apart for God and continually made holy. The imagination, both good and evil, is a frequently addressed concept in the Bible. The Hebrew word yêtser is found nine times in the Old Testament (Gen. 6:5; 8:21; Deut. 31:21; 1 Chron. 28:9; 29:18; Ps. 103:14; Isa. 26:3; 29:16; Hab. 2:18)."[11]

The imagination is often addressed in the Bible, along with the connotation that an imagination set apart for God creates a steadfast mind. The definition of steadfast is firmly fixed in place, immovable, not subject to change, firm in belief, determination, or adherence; loyal.[12] Another word often interchanged with steadfast is faithful. God is faithful to heal our minds.

### Applying the Scriptures

The key point to remember is that our imagination is to be dedicated to God and made holy by studying scripture, encountering Jesus, and applying these biblical truths to our lives. The activations in this devotional are meant to encourage you to use your imagination and invite Jesus, the Holy Spirit, or Father God to join you in an encounter. It starts with using your mind to visualize him standing, sitting, or hanging out beside you.

Each activation begins by engaging with the scripture for that day, allowing Jesus to speak to your heart and bring the personal healing and wholeness you need. He knows exactly what you need to hear to heal your heart. The beauty of these activations lies in their personal nature, involving God revealing his wisdom, grace, and extravagant love to you in a new and profound way, like only he can.

Here is my prayer for you, which is Paul's prayer from Ephesians 1, as you seek Jesus in the area of your imagination.

*"I pray that the Father of glory, the God of our Lord Jesus Christ, would impart to you the riches of the Spirit of wisdom and the Spirit of revelation to know him through your deepening intimacy with him. I pray that the light of God will illuminate the eyes of your imagination, flooding you with light, until you experience the full revelation of the hope of his calling —that is, the wealth of God's glorious inheritances that he finds in us, his holy ones!"*
Ephesians 1:17-18

## An Exercise for Imagination

If you have trouble imagining, here's a simple exercise:

Close your eyes and picture your kitchen. Imagine walking toward your refrigerator, opening the door, and picking up a food item. Hold it in your hand and set it on your counter. If you can imagine yourself doing these small tasks in your kitchen, you can also imagine yourself with Jesus. The best advice I received when I started this kind of encounter was not to overthink it.

Give it a try and let me know what happens!

## Prayer

*Father God,*

*Teach me how to dramatically change my way of thinking, use my imagination again, and become like a child so that I can see and hear you. I want to engage in this kind of encounter with you. Help me to stop overthinking and instead use my imagination to meet with you, Jesus, or the Holy Spirit. I want to see you and hear what you want to say about my grief journey. Please teach me how to draw near to you and hear your voice (John 10:27).*

*According to Ephesians 1:17-18, I pray that you, the Father of glory, the God of our Lord Jesus Christ, would give me the riches of the Spirit of wisdom and the Spirit of revelation to know you through my growing intimacy with you. I also pray that the light of God will illuminate the eyes of my imagination, flooding me with light, until I experience the full revelation of the hope of my calling—that is, the riches of your glorious inheritance in me, your holy one!*

*In Jesus' name, I pray,*
*Amen*

*"My own sheep will hear my voice and I know each one, and they will follow me."*
*John 10:27*

# About the Author

Rayna Piazza is a first-time author and a prayer intercessor dedicated to emotional healing, deepening intimacy with Jesus, and personal growth, all based on the biblical teachings of Jesus. After her husband's tragic suicide, she wrote this devotional. Rayna is dedicated to helping others heal their soul, break free from their past, and fulfill their divine purpose. She believes that the same power that raised Jesus from the dead (Romans 8:11) lives in her, and that you, too, can experience his power if you believe.

*"Yes, God raised Jesus to life! And since God's Spirit of Resurrection lives in you, he will also raise your dying body to life by the same Spirit that breathes life into you!"*
*Romans 8:11*

Jesus has taught Rayna how to dive into biblical truths to anchor her faith, renew her mind, and set her feet on solid ground. Through her writing, she shares these principles along with practical ways to apply them to your life. To walk in emotional wellness, you must first face your fears. Your emotional pain has a purpose. Rayna often says, "I like to think of the pain as a guide that shows me where Jesus wants to do his next work in me."

As you read Rayna's work, you'll learn to walk in union with Jesus through every season of your life. She writes for those who desire to fulfill their God-given destiny, even when they face fear, anxiety, or emotional pain. Rayna believes that God has a plan for you that involves thriving, flourishing, and fulfilling your God-given destiny. You were always meant to walk in emotional wellness.

Explore additional books and resources by Rayna at raynasbooks. com. Please leave a review on Amazon or Goodreads!

For motivation in your personal growth journey, visit Rayna's blog, seekinghimtoday.com, where she shares how to seek Jesus in today's world, along with her personal growth journals and this devotional, "When Grief Became My Gift," with more to come.

Stay connected on Instagram @raynasbooks for encouragement and updates on new releases.

# Endnotes

1 Day 7: "humility." Merriam-Webster.com. 2025. https://www.merriam-webster.com (12 September 2025)

2 Day 12: "forsake." Merriam-Webster.com. 2025. https://www.merriam-webster.com (12 September 2025)

3 Day 17: Emphasis mine, Brian Simmons, "Note on Matthew 5:3," in The Passion Translation: New Testament, ed. Brian Simmons, 15, note f (Nashville, TN: BroadStreet Publishing Group, 2020)

4 Day 20: Brian Simmons, "Note on Matthew 5:16," in The Passion Translation: New Testament, ed. Brian Simmons, 331, note h (Nashville, TN: BroadStreet Publishing Group, 2017)

5 Day 20: Simmons, "Note on Matthew 5:16," 17, 2020, note c

6 Day 24: Simmons, "Note on John 8:32," 610, 2017, note c

7 Day 28: Simmons, "Note on Hebrews 2:10," 1004, 2017, note d

8 Day 28: Simmons, "Note on Hebrews 2:10," 1004, 2017, note e

9 Day 39: Simmons, "Note on John 7:37," 606, 2017, note d

10 Day 39: Simmons, "Note on John 7:38," 606, 2017, note f

11 Appendix B: Brian Simmons, "Note on Isaiah 26:3," in The Passion Translation: The Book of Isaiah, ed. Brian Simmons, 64, note g (Nashville, TN: BroadStreet Publishing Group, 2019)

12 Appendix B: "steadfast." Merriam-Webster.com. 2025. https://www.merriam-webster.com (12 September 2025)

www.ingramcontent.com/pod-product-compliance
Lightning Source LLC
Chambersburg PA
CBHW060349090426
42734CB00011B/2088